ADVANCE PRAISE

The Story of a Hidden Child is a vivid, gripping portrayal of a Jewish family's attempts to survive the unspeakable horrors suffered throughout the Holocaust. The book is fortified by thorough historical research that provides rich, edifying context. More broadly, this book punctuates the timeless, enduring presence of deep-seated evil in our society, including the seemingly unimaginable ways it can take form.

This book is a powerful warning to Jews and other persecuted peoples—especially during these increasingly uncertain times—that apathy, inattention, and denial are wholly alien to our courage and our survival.

More broadly, this book punctuates the timeless, enduring presence of deep-seated evil in our society, including the seemingly unimaginable ways it can take form. This work is a powerful warning to Jews and other persecuted peoples—especially during these increasingly uncertain times—that apathy, inattention, and denial are wholly alien to our courage and our survival.

—Myles Martel, Ph.D.

Harry Pila unraveled astonishing mysteries when he investigated his parents' lives. The result is a deeply sensitive and impressively researched story of selflessness and bravery. The Journey of a Hidden Child is a powerful record of sacrifice and resistance in the face of terror.

—Keren Blankfeld, journalist and author.

THE JOURNEY OF A HIDDEN CHILD

HARRY PILA

ROBIN BLACK

ap

ISBN 9789493276567 (ebook)

ISBN 9789493276543 (paperback)

ISBN 9789493276550 (hardcover)

Publisher: Amsterdam Publishers, The Netherlands

info@amsterdampublishers.com

The Journey of a Hidden Child is part of the series Jewish Children in the Holocaust

Excerpts from Judy Cohen's *A Cry in Unison* (2020) used by permission of the publisher, The Azrieli Foundation.

Cover image: Helitha Nilmalgoda

CONTENTS

You haven't got a graveyard, convicted, but we keep your memory deep within our hearts and minds for always. And this will never be forgotten as long as we all shall live. The Jewish people will never forget. But the rest of the world — will they remember?

—Tobi Komornik-Gerson (1925-2008) Survivor of Auschwitz-Birkenau & Ravensbrück KL[1]

---

1. kehilalinks.jewishgen.org/szczercow/Memoir %20of %t20Tobi %20Komornik-Gerson.htm

PREFACE

Some of the details my mother shared with me about her life before the war turned out to be untrue, particularly regarding my biological father's religion. I uncovered the truth through research I conducted for this book, as well as by procuring the services of a Jewish Genealogy expert.

To learn, as I approach my 81st year, that almost everything I thought I knew about my birth father was false, including his name, rocked my perception of who I was. I do not know the reasons why my mother maintained the fictions about her past that included my father – happy years they spent together that were made all too brief by the Holocaust. Perhaps her need to preserve the fictions she created in the hopes that they would help us survive were difficult to part with. I learned the truth about my parents when I was nearing the completion of this book. It produced quite a conundrum. I had to rewrite whole chapters to weave this new information into an almost completed manuscript. The unique problem of starting a Holocaust memoir believing that the biggest hurdle were the gaps in the story, and not anticipating the inaccuracies in the scant knowledge that I *did* have is a story in itself. The steps I took to uncover the truth may help other Holocaust descendants learn about their own families' Holocaust histories.

Where there are gaps in my story, it is because I simply have no information, despite rigorous research. The Nazis burned millions of pages of records towards the end of the war in the attempt to hide the atrocities they committed in more than 1,000 concentration camps. At one point during the war there were 1,65 million registered prisoners.

I am guilty of not asking enough questions to those who are no longer here to solve a multitude of mysteries surrounding their pasts.

It is possible, however, to flesh out enough material for a book even if the subjects didn't tell a complete story, or, as in the case of my adoptive father, told one that was studded with inaccuracies and omissions. This was not uncommon, nor was it an attempt at obfuscation. Survivors gave testimonies of the most unspeakably painful years of their lives, often many decades after they lived through them. It was exceedingly brave of them to revisit the horrors they endured and witnessed so that future generations could extract the lessons to be learned from their experiences.

No one survivor's story is more important than another's. All the accounts are equally vital. Every chronicle of survival and non-survival is worth telling – the complete narratives and the not-so-complete ones. In the cases of my three parents, two biological and one adoptive, enough of their concentration camp records survived to allow me to fill in many of the missing details. I was able to find testimonies from survivors who were in the exact same place at the exact same time as my parents so that what they suffered was revealed to me in great detail. The websites of the camps, as well as scholarly books and articles, helped to further flesh out my parents' stories. When I was stuck, I reached out to historians working at the museums of the camps and to the United States Holocaust Memorial Museum (USHMM) in Washington, D.C. These historians are very happy to offer assistance so that the annals of proof of the most horrible chapter in human history continue to grow. As time moves ever further from the Holocaust, it is increasingly imperative that these stories remain a part of a global reckoning and conversation.

Soon we will lose the last survivors – the last subjects and eyewitnesses to the evil that man can visit upon man. Their testimonies must be passed down in the hopes that future generations will never allow history to repeat itself.

It is why I feel compelled to share all that I do know about my family's past. Mine is but one link in a heartbreakingly long chain. Every link is vitally important if decency and humanity are to prevail.

INTRODUCTION

I was born in Brussels, Belgium on March 15, 1941, to Rosa and Charles Russ. My parents were Polish Jews and 1941 was a precarious time for them to have a baby. Just ten months earlier, on May 28, 1940, Belgium had surrendered to the Nazis. Less than 18 months after my birth, the first groups of Jews were deported from Belgium to Auschwitz-Birkenau.

Despite my ill-timed arrival, I had a carefree early childhood. I am one of the lucky ones. I was a successfully hidden child. In the hopes of preserving my life, my parents had the foresight and emotional strength to give me away for safekeeping when I was only six weeks old. It was excruciating for them but crucial, and not just because they were Jewish. My parents were involved in the Resistance, having joined the Underground when the French capitulated to the Nazis on June 22, 1940. Rosa and Charles, already on shaky ground, further risked their lives, and mine by distributing anti-Nazi leaflets throughout Brussels. They are heroes to me.

My parents were fortunate in one regard. Unlike the anguished parents whose children were given to kind strangers or placed in orphanages and convents under assumed identities, my parents gave me to their best friends, a Gentile couple named Gerard and Germaine Decraene. Knowing where I was, that I was well, and even being able to visit me on occasion, gave my parents great peace of mind and periodic moments of joy.

Being so young, I was blissfully unaware of any of this. I had two loving "parents" and a comfortable home. The war was very far from my consciousness, even as I grew older.

1

RUCHLA

My mother, Ruchla Laja Sat, was born on November 28, 1911 in Szczerców, Poland. Her father, Henoch, was a weaver, her mother, Sura Bornstein Sat, was a homemaker. Ruchla joined her brother, Josef, nine, and sister, Zela, who was five. The family was middle class and strictly practiced Orthodox Judaism.

Szczerców was an unlucky place prone to repeated and calamitous fires. Possibly due to this, the family moved to the slightly larger town of Bełchatów, about 20 kilometers east of Szczerców and 40 kilometers north of Łódź, Poland's second largest city. Jews had been settling in and around Łódź since the late 18th century.

Like Szczerców, Bełchatów was a shtetl, a typical small Eastern European village with a large Jewish population. The rhythm of life in the shtetl was determined by tradition. News from the outside world rarely infiltrated the shtetl, and changes occurred incredibly slowly, if at all. The center of life was the synagogue, but in every shtetl there were also numerous houses of prayer where men gathered for religious practices and the study of the Talmud. Jews sought to preserve their religious, cultural, and external

1

distinctiveness through their different way of dressing. Upon marrying, women cut off their hair and wore wigs and hats. The men wore long black caftans and yarmulkes on their heads. Yiddish was the language of the Jews, preferred over the language of their home country. Yiddish is a fusion of about 80 percent German and 20 percent Hebrew, with many words incorporated from the Romance and Slavic languages, and in the last 100 years, from English as well. Written in Hebrew, Yiddish originated about 900 years ago. On Friday evenings in towns like Szczerców and Bełchatów, the gentle light of the Sabbath candles could be seen flickering through the curtains of Jewish homes. By 1939, according to the German Register, Jews made up 41 percent of Bełchatów's population. However, Jews actually constituted closer to 60 percent of the population because in their tally the Nazis had incorporated the populations of the surrounding villages, mostly Catholics and Protestants.

The textile industry drove the economic engine of interwar Łódź and its surrounding communities, including Bełchatów. The ready-made tailoring industry was almost entirely composed of Jews. Jewish merchants controlled wholesale and retail commerce in Łódź, marketing most of the textile production houses. Despite anti-Jewish policies enacted in the interwar period, Jews continued to work and prosper. In bigger towns especially, many became assimilated and abandoned the traditional dress and customs that had previously distinguished them from non-Jews.

Unfortunately, my grandmother Sura died before my mother reached her second birthday. Grandfather Henoch wasted no time in a new spouse to help him raise his three children, marrying a woman named Hinda Herschkovitz. Hinda promptly bore him a son, Jankiel Motek in 1914, followed by Frida Chana, Blima Golda. In 1924, Tzvi Herszel completed the family. My mother disliked Hinda because she favored her biological children over Josef, Zela, and herself,

2

giving them preferential treatment. Despite the inequity, Ruchla had an especially close relationship with her half-brother Jankiel.

In 1923, Zela moved out of the family home to marry a tailor named Fiszel Wajs. Ruchla was happy for her sister but missed her presence at home; the sisters were dear friends. Ruchla was delighted, however, when a year later Zela gave birth to a son, Abraham Wolf, who was born just four days before Herszel. Thus, the infant Abraham became an uncle before he reached the age of one week.

Three years later, Zela added a daughter to her family, whom she named Sura Rywka, after my grandmother. In 1929, the Wajs family relocated to Brussels, Belgium, where chances for advancement were beyond anything the couple could hope for in Poland. Ruchla missed her sister terribly. Though she didn't know it, the Wajs family's move to Belgium would change the trajectory of my mother's life forever.

In 1931, Ruchla was a 20-year-old still living in the crowded family home in Bełchatów. A bit of an outlier in her family's enthusiasm for religious Judaism, Ruchla was a spirited young woman who enjoyed an innocently good time. She was attractive, confident, and after devouring Zela's letters from Belgium, increasingly curious about the world outside of Poland. Zela was now employed as a seamstress in an upscale men's clothing store where Fiszel worked, right in the heart of Brussels. Zela might as well have been working on the moon; that's how different her life was from Ruchla's.

2

UNVEILING MY FATHER

For the entirety of my mother's life, the narrative she maintained about my father was that his original name was Serge de Russ, and that he was a Catholic Frenchman of Russian descent whose family had shortened their surname to Russ when they left Russia in the 19th century. She told me my father had been among a group of prisoners gunned down near the end of the war by a firing squad in a POW camp. According to my mother, she learned the events surrounding my father's death by the only man in the group to survive. He had climbed out physically unscathed from beneath the dead bodies after the shooters had left and reported the murders. This account, like others to be addressed in subsequent chapters, proved to be false.

When I started conducting research on my family for this book, what I learned shook me to my core. My father's first name was not Serge, he was not Catholic or French, and he was never in a POW camp. Rather, Szapsa Russ was born to Dawid Russ and Sura Dyna Russ neé Goldszmidt, in Piotrków Trybunalsi, Poland on May 5, 1908. He was the youngest of four brothers: Josek, born in 1900, Hersz, born in 1902, and Szmul Lejb, who arrived in 1905. Piotrków, a suburb of

Łódź, was part of Russia from 1815 to 1915 before reverting back to Poland in 1919.[1]

Piotrków was an important industrial center, principally for the manufacture of textiles, wood, and glass products. Jews had lived there since the early Middle Ages. By 1939, they numbered some 15,000 residents, making up approximately 27 percent of the total population. The thriving Jewish community, both secular and Orthodox, supported three weekly newspapers and numerous synagogues and prayer houses. Piotrków's Great Synagogue was considered one of the most beautiful buildings of its kind throughout Poland. The city was about 27 kilometers away from Bełchatów.

I have no information on how my parents met. However, on Tuesday, September 27, 1932, at 10 p.m., Rabbi Mendel Weiss officiated in their religious marriage ceremony. In the civil marriage certificate filed in Piotrków on November 10, 1932, both Szapsa and Ruchla were listed as tailors. (Perhaps they met through their shared occupation.) The document also listed both of Ruchla's parents as deceased. Szapsa's parents were still living, although his brother Szmul Lejb had died in 1928. None of his surviving brothers or Ruchla's siblings were among the recorded witnesses at the nuptials.

---

1. Claims that my father was of Russian descent may have stemmed from this fact.

3

NEW BEGINNINGS FOR RUCHLA AND SZAPSA

The young couple was undoubtedly making plans for their future before they wed, and it didn't include a life in Poland. Only six days after their marriage, Szapsa had a Polish official draw up a Certificate of Morality to augment his application to gain legal status in another country. Soon after, he traveled to Paris. Ruchla remained in Poland. Szapsa stayed at the house of someone named Jaklovic for a short time, perhaps a friend from Poland. Then he entered Belgium with his Polish passport. It was written in his file that he had failed to apply for a visa beforehand. It was also noted that he was a cutter who specialized in the field of patternmaking. Paradoxically, Szapsa told the Belgian authorities that he had the intention of opening a bakery with an associate named Raphael Goldman. He also stated that he did not know how long he planned to stay in the country. If his permission to remain in Belgium were to be rejected, his intention, he wrote, would be to try gaining entry into Germany. Learning that killed any assumption that my parents were leaving Poland, at least in part, due to antisemitism.

During this period, Szapsa lived on 50,000 francs (about $1,000) in savings. On September 21, 1933, he asked the authorities to approve his travel to Paris, which was needed so he could be granted readmission into Belgium. He spent seven months in Paris before returning to Brussels. In April 1934, after a separation of 18 months, Ruchla traveled to Belgium for a reunion with Szapsa so they could apply for visas together. For unknown reasons, both were denied. My mother returned to Poland alone, while my father remained as an illegal resident. Five months later, he was arrested for overstaying his visa. He was also thought of as a drain on the government, since he didn't have firm employment. From Verviers Prison, he was to be escorted to a train station in another city, where he would need to board a train for Poland within 24 hours. Once he was on the train, he would be given a certificate of freedom.

Szapsa never got on the train. He rectified his unemployment situation by securing a job at Kaytan Frères, the men's clothing store that Uncle Fiszel managed and where Aunt Zela worked as a seamstress.[1] On May 29, 1935, my father's persistence and sheer chutzpah paid off. A government official issued him a work permit valid through May 31, 1936, writing: "I have the honor of letting you know that I have examined the contract of work from Caton [sic] Frères." Having risked expulsion from the country, Szapsa was fastidious in reapplying for a new work permit every six months.

Fortunes finally reversed for my parents, who had barely spent more than a few nights together since their wedding. Ruchla received her Certificate of Morality on November 5, 1935, having traveled to the Belgian consulate in Warsaw to apply for a visa to join her husband permanently to "be a housewife." She presumably joined him in Brussels, because, according to their file, the Belgian government wanted to kick *both* of them out of the country soon after, claiming not to have received Szapsa's certificate of employment. My parents reapplied for an extension and considered emigrating to Argentina for its open-door policy. Before they could crack the binding on a Spanish-Polish dictionary, however, the Belgians extended their visas. Interestingly, Szapsa put in a request for readmittance into Belgium in July 1939 so he could travel to Poland to "see his old mother."[2] There is no record to indicate that Ruchla ever went back to Poland after moving to Belgium. Every year, my parents kept up with the visa application system, which gave them permission to stay in Belgium until January 1942.

My mother was enthralled by her new country. Belgium was a small yet diverse country of great plains and gently rolling land, hills, lakes, rivers, and canals. The seashore, with its 67 kilometers of pristine, sandy beaches, beckoned vacationers and citizens alike to a climate that was never harsh even though it often rained. It was a place rich in resources: fertile land, coal, and a long tradition of master craftsmen and fine workmanship. Brussels had even hosted the World's Fair the year before. Here, cars and buses rolled down the streets in stark contrast to the pushcarts that choked the market square of Bełchatów. Even Zela seemed more exotic to Ruchla after being gently reshaped by seven years of city living. She had even shed her Yiddish name in favor of the more sophisticated, Western European *Celina*, the German version of the French *Céline*.

Jews in Eastern European countries like Poland differed greatly from those in Western European countries such as Belgium. Western Jews were far more assimilated. They dressed and spoke the same language as their non-Jewish neighbors, and traditional religious practices and Yiddish culture generally played a less important role in their lives. Ruchla had learned rudimentary French in Poland, and once she was settled in Brussels, my cousin Sura coached her in the language until she was fluent. As Celina had done, Ruchla replaced her Yiddish name with *Rosa*. Szapsa had already traded his old name to Charles.

The time my father spent outside of Poland yielded a more sophisticated man. Szapsa/Charles had never been conventionally attractive. He had a receding hairline and protruding ears. But he dressed like a page from a fashion magazine now, and carried an omnipresent cigarette between his fingers. To Ruchla/Rosa, he was still the extremely kind and sincere man she had married. But he now had a suaveness to him that he hadn't had before. He even had stylish friends. His new best friend was Gerard Decraene, a professor of Men's Fabrics and Fashion at the Free University of Brussels. Gerard's expertise in men's fashion patternmaking had brought Charles into his social circle. Gerard's wife, Germaine, quickly took Rosa under her wing, and the four became very close.

---

1. My mother maintained that my father owned the store, although this is highly unlikely.
2. Had he visited her the following month and stayed in the country until at least September 1st, when the Nazis invaded Poland, the border would have been closed.

4

———

WAR

Charles and Rosa settled in Schaerbeek, a stylish, upscale municipality of Brussels. Their visa troubles behind them, they were finally enjoying their life together when they were jolted to the grim reality of the world outside of Belgium. Germany invaded Poland on September 1, 1939. In response, Poland's allies Great Britain and France declared war on Germany two days later. My parents and aunt and uncle were worried for their families in Bełchatów and Piotrków. Eastern Europe seemed so very far away from Belgium, a neutral country and therefore immune to the events consuming England, France, Poland, and Czechoslovakia.[1] For a time, life continued relatively unchanged in Belgium. The happiness my parents experienced in their personal life made the war seem like a distant, bad dream.

The fantasy that the war would bypass Belgium evaporated when the Nazis invaded Western Europe. The country's neutrality was shattered. As part of their strategy to defeat Great Britain and France, the Wehrmacht [the German army] invaded Belgium on May 10, 1940. Just before 5 a.m. German *Stukas* [dive bombers] began their campaign flying "neatly in rows, as if it were an exercise," recalled one Belgian. Residents looked out their windows to see the sky blackened by dark shapes raining down on the still sleeping city. One witness described seeing two manned dive bombers having a field day as people on the streets ran for shelter when they heard the "dreadful whirring sound of those planes."

The Belgian Prime Minister, Paul Reynaud, attempted to reassure his citizens by reminding them: "We have the Albert Canal, and they will not pass." His radio broadcasts were memorable, not only because they sadly miscalculated the German military's strength but, as he was appealing to Belgians to remain strong, parachutists were dropping into the country to seize its utilities.

After 18 days of fighting, King Leopold surrendered the Belgian army and capitulated to the Germans. Jews living in Belgium numbered an estimated 66,000 out of a population of eight million. Fewer than ten percent were Belgian citizens, the vast majority consisting of immigrants and refugees who had fled the persecution after Hitler's attack on Poland. Many were craftsmen, merchants, or workers who lived very modestly. A small number of them worked in the diamond business in Antwerp, whereas in Brussels the majority were employed in textiles and leather or trades related to those fields. Many of them still spoke Yiddish and clung to their old-world traditions. An estimated 15,000 to 20,000 Jewish refugees from the Reich entered Belgium between 1933 and 1939.

Many Belgians, not just Jews, were gripped with deadly fear. Those who had lived through World War I were still afflicted with the emotional scars they had acquired from the atrocities inflicted upon them by the German army in that war. The Germans had invaded neutral Belgium on August 4, 1914 in order to outflank the French army. The following day, Belgian civilians were executed as the invading Germans advanced on their first hurdle, a ring of forts around Liège. To retaliate for the Belgians' defensive shelling from these forts, the German troops had rounded up the inhabitants of surrounding villages and shot them. For the victims who hadn't died, the Germans used bayonets to finish them off. In four days, nearly 850 civilians had been killed. By the end of October that figure was more than 5,500. In 1914 alone, the Germans destroyed 25,000 homes and buildings and 837 communities. They imprisoned ordinary citizens and installed lethal electric fences to prevent civilians from fleeing the country, killing 3,000. A staggering 120,000 Belgians were deported for forced labor, half of them to Germany. Twenty percent of the population, 1,5 million Belgians, had fled from the invading Wehrmacht during World War I.

But that had been over a quarter century before. The German army of 1940 was more disciplined than its predecessor of 1914. There was just one massacre, in the Flemish city of Vinkt, in retaliation for the Belgian army's continued resistance. The Wehrmacht took hostages and used them as human shields, executing many civilians outright before Belgium's surrender on May 28.

Paul Struye, publisher of the clandestine *La Libre Belgique* [The Free Belgium] even wrote in his diary: "During the first months there really was no enmity to be detected between the population and the army. It was a pleasant surprise for the Belgians to see the German soldiers, correct in their attitude and other behavior. They had nothing in common with the imperial troops of 1914-1918. Belgium was occupied by an army in which order and discipline reigned without outrages."

Within days of Belgian's entry into the war, Rosa learned she was pregnant. My parents digested the news with mixed feelings. They had not been trying for a baby. They were overjoyed to be having a child, but who in their right mind brought a new life into such uncertain and dangerous times? Especially a Jewish baby.

---

1. The latter country had been partially annexed by the Nazis in 1938 and invaded by them the previous March.

5

___

ANTI-JEWISH MEASURES IN BELGIUM & RESISTANCE

Soon after the invasion, a military administration was established for Belgium under the command of Wehrmacht general Alexander von Falkenhausen, who in turn appointed SS officer Eggert Reeder as the head of the military government for civil matters, including the treatment of Jews. The administration adopted anti-Jewish policies with the ultimate aim of eradicating the Jewish presence in Belgium. The German tactic regarding the Jewish population was divided into two discrete phases: the Preparatory phase and the Deportation phase. The Nazis launched the first anti-racial policies on October 28, 1940. If Belgium's Jews had held any illusions that they would be safe in a previously neutral country, those fragile hopes began to erode.

The first set of restrictions was pervasive: a ban on kosher slaughtering practices, the dismissal of Jews from government employment, including teachers and professors, and the banning of Jews from the fields of journalism and law. Anyone who had three or four Jewish grandparents was considered Jewish, according to the laws. Whether these individuals practiced Judaism or not was irrelevant to the Nazis. Even those who descended from grandparents who had converted to Christianity decades before were considered Jewish, and all of them would be forced to register with the Belgian authorities to have their identification cards stamped in red ink with the word JUIF.

Jews rushed to register themselves and their families at the town hall for fear of severe penalties for non-compliance. My parents, however, waited two months before adding their names to the register on December 27, 1940. Had they been weighing their options during this time? My mother never spoke of it. Belgium's Jews hoped they might be allowed to stay in the country if they kept quiet and obeyed the Nazis. The only apparent alternative – an extremely dangerous one – was to flee. But how, and to where? Jewish-owned businesses also had to register, and publicly patronized businesses, such as hotels, cafes, and restaurants, needed to be identified as such with a sign in their windows.

And then, some much-needed good news.

On October 31, 1940, the Britain's Royal Air Force [RAF] caused extensive damage to the *Luftwaffe* [German air force], ending the Nazi bombing campaign that had begun on September 7, known as the *Blitz*. By the last day of October, more than 1,700 German planes had been destroyed, compared to just over 900 RAF plans. It was a much-needed victory for England and the allies. With Germany's first major setback, Belgians began to shift from the belief that Germany was invincible. This change in attitude, combined with the population's growing antipathy towards the Germans, brought a change of mood and offered resistance fertile ground to form. Resistance groups soon sprang up throughout the country. Men and women began sabotaging the Germans' military infrastructure and assassinating Nazi collaborators. As many as 40,000 Belgians were involved with the underground press alone, printing 567 separate newspapers. My parents, along with their best friends, the Decraenes, were quick to join the movement, becoming part of an organization primarily made up of non-Jews. Charles and a heavily pregnant Rosa began distributing anti-Nazi leaflets. They were aware of the risks they were taking, but as soon-to-be-parents to a Jewish child, standing by and letting others take on a fight that was deeply personal to them was out of the question.

6

NAZI PERSECUTION IN EUROPE

Rosa and Celina stayed apprised of the events in Poland as best they could. When the Nazis occupied Bełchatów on September 9, 1939, many Jewish homes, stores, and factories went up in smoke as a result of the shelling. When the Jews fled the city in haste, the Gentile inhabitants grabbed anything of value that was left behind. The Jews who remained in the town were immediately brutalized by the Nazis, their possessions plundered. The Nazis tortured them emotionally as well as physically, forcing them to gather and bury all the corpses from the area. They ordered Jewish men to wrap themselves in their prayer shawls and parade through the city, making them dance, sing, and proclaim slogans such as: "We Jews are war criminals." They carried them through the streets on ladders, then flung them to the ground. Jews were pushed off rooftops and beaten until bloody.

Special persecutions increased during the High Holy Days of Rosh Hashanah, the Jewish New Year, and Yom Kippur, the Day of Atonement. While praying quietly, Jews were dragged out of their homes and made to work loathsome jobs. One group was forced to sweep up horse manure in the market square, collect it in their hands and put it in their pockets and caps. Torahs and synagogues were set on fire. Bełchatówer Jews were forced to trample on sacred religious scrolls and texts collected during house-to-house searches. As the holy tracts were set on fire, they were ordered to dance and sing around the bonfire. It was so large, it burned for days. Field kitchens were brought to the marketplace, where the Nazi's non-kosher rations were shoved down the throats of elderly Jews. Some of the mens' beards were shaved with bayonets, while others were made to hold hot coals in their hands. Many Gentile Bełchatówers and *Volksdeutsche* [ethnic Germans] gleefully participated in the persecutions of their Jewish neighbors.

Identical barbarities by the Nazis were performed in shtetls across Poland. In Widawa, where the rabbi refused to burn Jewish holy books, they burned him alive as he held the Torah in his hands. In Będzin, home to more than 20,000 Jews, 200 of them were driven into a synagogue where Nazis locked the door and set it on fire. In my father's hometown of Piotrków, Jewish men were arrested and ordered to clean the city's streets and public laboratories with their prayer shawls.

Charles, Rosa, Celina, and Fiszel most likely knew what was happening in Poland. Despite the chaos, the post was still functioning. The following excerpt is from a letter received in England from a relative, a teenaged girl living in Warsaw:

"For the killing of one German, whole massacres among the Poles are being perpetrated every day and in general shooting of people goes on constantly for the most trivial reasons, as well as putting them to prison. Tens of thousands of completely innocent people are filling the prisons. In spite of it all Warsaw is as a paradise compared to Pomerania (area of Poland near the Baltic Sea) or Posnania (area in northwest Poland) where the people are being driven out of their dwelling places and not allowed to take anything with them. Then they put them into unheated trucks and leave them somewhere in the open country in this cold. Untold horrors are being done with the Jews."

7

NEW ANTI-JEWISH MEASURES

Ten months after Belgium surrendered to the Nazis, I was born in a hospital in Ixelles, Belgium, on March 15, 1941. My parents were thrilled to have a healthy son. I was a fat, roly-poly infant topped with a full head of wavy, dark hair. My parents understandably chose for me a very Christian name: Jean-Pierre. My arrival was a joyous distraction for them, the Wajs family, and the Decraenes. My mother cheerfully succumbed to all the duties of new motherhood and tried to shut out the events surrounding her, which was becoming increasing harder to do when the Nazis enacted a second round of anti-Jewish policies. Now, Jews were forced to register their real estate holdings. Any sale of real estate was subject to German approval; any monies from sales had to be deposited into special bank accounts. The Germans also confiscated all radio sets belonging to Jews. It was the third sanction, however, that really hit home: Jews were banned from management jobs in business. Fiszel had to give up managing Kaytan, though he was able to retain employment at the store in a lesser position.

Soon the Nazis tightened the noose for all Belgians, regardless of their religion. The country's citizens grew even more resentful of the

Germans when they announced a succession of new decrees, such as the suspension of municipal and provincial councils, and the implementation of a curfew. According to one Belgian women, it seemed that every time a German officer was killed, a curfew was instituted for the whole civilian population. Everybody had to be inside between 10 p.m. and 6 a.m. A month later, the Nazis ordered a stricter curfew for the Jews: 8 p.m. to 7 a.m.

But when the Germans set Belgian food rations to roughly two-thirds of what German citizens were allocated, the Belgians turned wholly against them, increasing the desire for a flourishing Resistance. In 1939, the typical diet of a Belgian miner, for example, had 700 grams of bread, butter or margarine, eggs or cheese, with meat and fruit for his lunch. In 1941, this was reduced to three slices of bread and a little jam. The food restriction was partly due to the increasing demands on the German economy, stemming from their invasion of the Soviet Union in June 1941, just two months after my birth.

The lowest point for Belgians regarding rationing came when the Germans decreed that each occupied country had to not only feed themselves, but also their hated German occupying force. This proved most daunting, as the amount of grain imported annually into the country abruptly ceased. One Belgian recalled: "For the first couple of years, [we] also had to deal with the shortage or the total absence of food. Most of the cows had to be killed by the farmers, as they could not feed them. Therefore, there was no milk for adults, only for small children, no butter, no margarine and no cheese. There was, of course, no meat. The butchers' shops displayed cardboard cutouts of cuts of meat. Bread was still obtainable, but the flour was adulterated by the addition of other things like crushed sugar beet, which made the bread sweet and sticky and upset most people's digestion."

Adding to the food crisis was the dwindling fish and seafood supply. As the Wehrmacht closed in on Belgian ports, many fishermen carried their family and friends away to England for the duration of the war. This reduced the fishing fleet, thus diminishing a vital source of food.

It wasn't just the restrictions on food that provided a strong basis for resistance organizations. Fuel and clothes were also in limited supply. Clandestine newspapers used the shortages as a call to arms to their readers. These shortages were often presented as proof that the Germans were ransacking the occupied countries.

8

A HIDDEN CHILD

Being involved in the Resistance was perilous enough. Being a Jew in the Resistance was a death wish. The punishments the Nazis doled out didn't end with the people they caught – they extended the bloodshed to their families as well. Therefore, when I was about six weeks old, my parents made the painful and unselfish decision to hide me in plain sight under the care of Gerard and Germaine Decraene. It was too dangerous for them to keep me, and there was no way they were going to quit their important resistance work. What they were fighting for was greater than their anguish from our separation. They were actively trying to make the world a safer place for me and any future children they might have. The luxury of keeping their baby seemed small in comparison. This long visit was ostensibly to spend the last months of her pregnancy and subsequent recuperation from childbirth. For my mother, hiding me was an easy decision. She knew it was a question of , not if she would be caught. Even though Gerard and Germaine were also involved in the resistance, I was safer under their roof, they thought.

Caring for a newborn indefinitely was a considerable favor for my parents to ask of their friends. The presence of a Jewish child in a private home represented constant danger. An infant offered a unique dilemma: how to explain the existence of a new family member when Germaine had never appeared pregnant. But the Decraenes didn't hesitate for a minute. They were willing to risk their lives by hiding me. They decided that the best course of action was to outwardly flaunt me, to take me for walks to the park and proudly show me off, rather than trying to keep my existence under wraps, which would seem suspicious. But first, as soon as I was entrusted in their care, Germaine whisked me off to a farm in Vilvoorde, a small country town about an hour by streetcar from Schaerbeek, that was owned by Gerard's mother and stepfather.

After a few months, she triumphantly returned to the city to show off the miracle of her late-in-life bundle of joy. The plan was a success. Playing the role of delighted new parents was no acting job for the Decraenes. Germaine had been unable to conceive due to a streetcar accident during her teenage years. She and Gerard genuinely fell in love with me. To augment my status as their biological child, Gerard used some connections to acquire a forged birth certificate stating my name as Jean-Pierre Decraene.

Fortunately, we lived close enough to my parents that they could visit me as regularly as safety permitted. Charles and Rosa were unaware of how intensely the Decraenes were involved with anti-Nazi activities. That intelligence was too dangerous for them to share with anyone, let alone my parents. The reality was that I was only marginally safer as their "son."

One of the Resistance's most urgent missions was to help the British, American, and Canadian airmen who'd been shot down in Belgium or just outside its borders to evade capture by the enemy. There were over 20 separate escape lines, and Belgium was a big player, along with France, the Netherlands, and Denmark. The leaders of the escape lines relied on networks of volunteers to find the downed pilots, feed and clothe them, manufacture false identity papers, and hide them in their homes. The Decraenes were deeply entrenched in this work and sheltered about 15 pilots in their attic during the war. One of them, Tom Wilkinson, was so grateful to the Decraenes that he maintained a close relationship with them, even coming to Belgium periodically for visits years after the war.

To get the pilots safely back to England, Gerard brought Tom and the other pilots he hid to Koksijde, a Belgian coastal town on the North Sea, where they waited for the fishing boats traveling back and forth between the two countries to sail to the coast of the town and signal their location. Then Gerard and the pilots swam or used a rubber dinghies to get to the boats. As a decoy, the boats were loaded with fish. If they were stopped by the Nazis, they could pass as working fishing boats, which they were. Nobody in Gerard's network was ever caught, but some missions were aborted when Germans were spotted patrolling the beaches.

9

THE NOOSE TIGHTENS

The Nazi system of pernicious discrimination was perfectly planned from a psychological standpoint. Their approach was to exercise moderation in their persecution of the Jews of Western European because they had to consider the sentiments of the general population, whom they hoped to win over to the "New Order." Furthermore, antisemitism was not as rabid in countries like Belgium as it was in Eastern European countries such as Poland and the Ukraine, where the Nazis could count on many of the local populations to enthusiastically partner with them in their persecutions.

In Belgium, the earliest anti-Jewish ordinances were designed to avoid overtly upsetting the general population. Indeed, the prohibition of kosher slaughter failed to garner attention from most non-Jews and was not a hardship for the country's many non-religious Jews. The next mandate, making Jews register their religion with a red stamp on their official papers, also failed to alarm the population. And the ban on commercial jobs for Jews meant less competition in the job market for the Gentiles. But the Resistance was growing. The hate against the Germans, who scorned Belgium's neutrality, made them want to fight against their occupiers with all their might.

Since Belgium's constitution did not allow data collection on religion, the German occupation authorities had to construct their own incomplete registry, which they created with the assistance of an organization they established in December 1941 for this purpose: *Association des Juifs en Belgique* (AJB). An executive board was appointed and the chief rabbi of Belgium, Rabbi Salomon Ullmann, was chosen as its chairman. The Nazis aimed to utilize the AJB to facilitate the implementation of their anti-Jewish orders. To make sure the register was complete, the Nazis decreed that every Jew must be a member of the AJB. Under the constant control of the SS officer responsible for Jewish affairs, the AJB became the Jewish tool through which the political police were able, in a peaceful manner, to gather up the first almost 4,000 Jews sent away for "compulsory labor," which sounded much less frightening than "deportation to a concentration camp." Subsequently, the *Sipo-SD* [Security Police] undertook the administration of an assembly camp in the city of Mechelen.[1] From its inception, the Jews of Belgium distrusted the AJB. The organization was officially portrayed as the governing body representing and caring for the needs of the Jewish community. But in reality, its main function was to gather the country's Jews to the SS Assembly camp for forced labor and deportations to Auschwitz. The register was arranged by household. Heads of families, each member of the family, and even Jewish maids from Eastern Europe were listed. Based on this data, the Gestapo created their files, which took up ten square meters of metal filing cabinets – data relating to the 56,168 men, women, and children who met the Nazi criteria as Jewish. Each Jew had a folder with a description sheet, to which was added other documents from other registers, so that slowly but surely, a small file was prepared for each person.

Nazi oppression picked up speed in 1942. The new year brought new bans. Jews were now forbidden to leave the country. In early

March, the Germans instituted a general labor draft, subjecting the Jews of Belgium to forced labor. A total of 2,252 Jews were sent to build fortifications along the coast of northern France. They were very quickly exhausted by the hard labor and mistreatment. The brutality of the guards caused many deaths. A few inmates managed to escape, thanks to the help of sympathetic Belgians living in the region who were willing to take the risk, but most escapees succeeded by their own means.

Having eliminated the Jews publicly, economically, and culturally, the Nazis were gearing up for their final opus: the deportation of every Jew in Belgium.

On January 20, 1942, 15 high-ranking Nazi and government officials, including Adolf Eichmann, gathered at an elegant villa in the Berlin suburb of Wannsee for a meeting chaired by Reinhard Heydrich, the chief of the Reich Security Main Office. The meeting's agenda was to discuss the implementation of the *Final Solution of the Jewish Question*, the plan for the systematic deportation and genocide of the entire population of European Jewry. The meeting would become known as the Wannsee Conference. In Eastern European countries with high Jewish populations, such as Poland, most Jews had already been forced to live in squalid and grossly overcrowded ghettos from which they could easily be transported to the extermination camps in the east. But in Western Europe, although Jews lived in strained circumstances, they were at least able to remain in their own homes. That would soon change.

---

1. It can also be spelled Mecheln. In French, the city is known as Malines.

10

YELLOW STAR

The last two measures of Phase One, the so-called Preparatory phase of anti-Jewish laws, came in May 1942. All Jews, beginning with children ages six years and older, were ordered to wear a yellow Star of David patch with a black letter J in its center. The star had to be displayed prominently on all Jews' outer clothing when in public. For those who failed to comply, there were harsh penalties. This was the most visual of the persecutions, and it triggered a sharp awareness among most Belgian citizens. Jews could now be easily identified. Before the yellow star, Belgians were largely indifferent to the fate of the Jews. Now they were shocked. If none of the previous antisemitic acts failed to evoke the population's sympathy, this one did. On the street, many people greeted Jews to show their solidarity. The work of Gentile resistance workers became more personal. They weren't just fighting on behalf of their country anymore, but for a persecuted people. The yellow star made the Jews vulnerable and sometimes, especially in Antwerp, subject to physical and verbal attacks by local collaborators and antisemites. It also aided the Nazis in identifying Jews in crowds and arresting them.

My parents refused to wear the star.

The cunning restraint with which the Nazis doled out their laws had been crafted to make the Jews hope that each persecution would be the last. As you read this book from the (relative) safety of the 21st century, you probably want to scream: "Get out! Don't be naive!" But you have the benefit knowing the events of the past. This is probably not the first book about the Holocaust you've read. And if it is, you've hopefully already learned about it in school. Unfortunately, because of what you already know about the Holocaust, and because genocide continues into this century, albeit not as methodically as the Nazis practiced it, it fails to shock you the way that it should.

Try to imagine it is 1942 and you are a Jew living in Belgium. The gears of slaughter are just beginning to turn in places like Auschwitz-Birkenau. There is no television or internet to disseminate the horror happening in distant Poland. Had you been my mother or father, would you, in your wildest visions, have fathomed the ultimate plans the Nazis had to eradicate the entire Jewish population? Plans to deport millions of people throughout Europe to extermination centers where their murders were engineered with the most extreme efficiency? Who could have imagined such expertly planned and executed evil?

In the summer of 1942, the Bund, a Jewish labor organization, got word to London that 700,000 Polish Jews had been murdered in 1941. The BBC took the story seriously. The US State Department, however, doubted a later report it received that Nazi Germany had adopted a policy to resolve the Jewish question with the murder of up to four million Jews by of poison gas. That information had been dispatched by anti-Nazi industrialists through intermediaries to the World Jewish Congress in Switzerland, and from there to London and Washington. Even in the fall of 1942 there was considerable resistance in Washington to the conclusion that the Nazis were singling Jews out for extermination. The story was so fantastical, so beyond the scope of evil, that the US government didn't believe it.

On June 1, 1942, a Warsaw underground newspaper, the *Liberty Brigade*, shared the news of the gassing of tens of thousands of Jews at Chełmno, a Nazi death camp in Poland. One young Jew, Emanuel Ringelblum, had succeeded in escaping after being forced to bury bodies as they were thrown out of gas vans. The West now knew the "bloodcurdling news... about the slaughter of Jews."

Ten days later, Adolf Eichmann, the architect of the Final Solution, convened a meeting with the heads of the Jewish Affairs Department in France, Belgium, and the Netherlands. Here, the plans for the extermination of European Jewry were set in motion. Beginning that same day, the Nazis began the systematic murder of the Jews of Tarnów, Poland, a town approximately 70 kilometers east of Kraków. The slaughter lasted for the next eight days. First, thousands of Jews were forced to report to the market square, during which time 3,000 people were shot in the streets and at the Jewish cemetery. Seven thousand more people were murdered in a nearby forest. The mass killings were not enough to stanch the Nazis' zeal for murder; twelve thousand more were taken to the Bełżec death camp, where they were summarily liquidated.

11

PSEUDO-SCIENTIFIC MEDICINE

In June 1942, an SS *Oberführer* [senior leader] named Viktor Brack wrote a letter to Heinrich Himmler, the Commander in Chief of the SS:

Among tens of millions of Jews in Europe, there are, I figure, at least two to three millions of men and women who are fit enough to work. Considering the extraordinary difficulties the labor problem presents us with, I hold the view that those two to three millions should be specially selected and preserved. This can, however, only be done if at the same time, they are rendered incapable to propagate.

After receiving Brack's letter, Himmler ordered sterilization experiments to be conducted on prisoners in Auschwitz. Birkenau was the extermination branch of the Auschwitz camp system, where the bulk of the incoming prisoners were immediately killed in the gas chambers. Those selected for labor were usually worked to death. Birkenau had an average life expectancy rate of three weeks. With Auschwitz's unlimited pool of newcomers (the Auschwitz Museum claims almost 1,1 million deportees were sent there) it was an ideal place from which to draw subjects for experimentation. Dovetailing perfectly with Brack's request was one from Professor Dr. Carl Clauberg, a gynecologist whose research specialty was, ironically, studying treatments to help infertile women conceive. A fanatical Nazi, Clauberg had a banner year in 1933 when he had joined the Nazi Party *and* been appointed Professor of Gynecology at the University of Königsberg. Clauberg approached Himmler, who was familiar with his work, only a month before Himmler received Brack's letter. Clauberg was looking for an opportunity to perform sterilization experiments on a broad scale. It was a serendipitous merging of intents for all involved parties. Two months later, on July 7, 1942, Himmler informed Dr. Clauberg that Auschwitz was at his disposal for experiments on animals and humans. The SS Chief asked for a report on the results of the experiments once they were concluded in order to begin the practical use of sterilization of Jewish women. In a memo Brack wrote up after meeting with Himmler, he noted: "It should also be examined, preferably in cooperation with Professor Dr. Hohlfelder, an X-ray specialist in Germany, what way sterilization of men could be achieved by X-ray treatment."

The results gleaned from the experiments were to yield a slave population incapable of reproducing. For Himmler, that was just one goal. He was also interested in procuring a method to carry out the biological destruction of all nations. The Nazis referred to all non-Aryan populations as life unworthy of life.

Before Clauberg's work could commence in Auschwitz, however, Himmler summoned him to Ravensbrück, the only concentration camp exclusively for women, to perform studies on how much time was needed to effectively sterilize 1,000 Jewish women. By the end of December 1942, Clauberg was back in Auschwitz. He performed his first experiments in Birkenau on a few female prisoners furnished to him for his sole disposal on December 28, 1942.

On April 3, 1943, Clauberg's entire "medical" team was moved to a two-story brick building in Block 10 of Auschwitz I, the main camp. It was separated from block 11 by a courtyard where mass shootings of prisoners regularly took place at the Death Wall, a structure equipped with cork plates to catch the bullets. On the ground floor of Block 10 were two large hospital rooms, an X-ray room, an operating theater, an office of the dentistry station, the hygiene institute, a room for the nurses, a room for an SS woman, and a bathroom and toilets. The upper floor had the capacity to house between 500 to 700 female prisoners. The windows of the building were permanently shuttered to prevent the women from witnessing the executions at the Death Wall. The lights were often left off in the unheated rooms, leaving the women shivering in total darkness.

Clauberg's inclusion criteria for his subjects consisted of married females between the ages of 20 and 40, preferably those who had given birth, ensuring they had no infertility issues.[1] A mere six months after he began his experiments in Auschwitz, he wrote obsequiously to Himmler:

"July 7, 1943

Dear Reichsführer,

Today I am fulfilling my obligation to report to you from time to time about the state of my research work. In doing this I am, as before, adhering to the procedure to report only if the matter is essential. The fact that after my most recent interview in July 1942 I could not do so before today is due to temporary difficulties in detail against which I myself was powerless, and with which I could not bother you, Reichsführer. I mention as an example that only since February 1943 am I in possession of an X-ray installation, which is of urgent value to my special research. In spite of the short period of actually only four months, it is already today possible to report to you, Reichsführer the following:

The method I contrived, to achieve the sterilization of the female organism without any operation is as good as perfected. It can be performed by a single injection made from the entrance of the uterus in the course of the usual customary gynecologic examinations known to every physician. If I say that the method is 'as good as perfected,' this means:

1. Still to be worked out are minor improvements of the method.
2. Already today it could be put to practical use in the course of our regular eugenic sterilizations and could thus replace the operation.

As to the question which you, Reichsführer, asked me almost one year ago, i.e. how much time would probably be required to sterilize 1,000 women by using this method: Today I can answer you with regard to the future as follows:

If my research continues to have the same results as up to now, and there is no reason to doubt that, then at the moment it is no longer far off when I can say:

By one adequately trained physician in one adequately equipped place with perhaps 10 assistants (the number of assistants in conformity with the desired acceleration) most likely 700 – if not even 1,000 per day."

My mother, in her early thirties when she arrived at Auschwitz, was unfortunately a perfect subject for Clauberg.

---

1. A small number of Clauberg's subjects were post-menopausal so he could attempt to reintroduce fertility by implanting the older women with ovaries.

12

MECHELEN/MALINES

Roughly 30 kilometers north of Brussels, in the Flemish city of Mechelen, stands a former army facility, the General Dossin de Saint-Georges barracks. During the war, it was referred to more simply as the Kaserne Dossin, Malines, or Mechelen.[1] The four wings of the three-story quarters formed a perfect rectangle with a courtyard in the center from which nobody on the outside could see in. It was also conveniently located between the major cities of Antwerp and Brussels, where 90 percent of Belgium's Jews lived. It had the perfect infrastructure to contain a great number of these Jews to fill many convoys to the east. On July 25, 1942, Malines opened as an official Nazi Assembly camp.

As the barracks was being readied for its inaugural prisoners, the Chief of Military Administration summoned Jews through a letter, delivered through the AJB, on the pretext of deportation for labor mobilization:

(Name, birthday, address) must arrive immediately for deployment for work.

You must therefore report on (date) by 12:00 o'clock to the assembly camp Mecheln Dossin-barracks.

You should depart early to ensure your arrival at the designated time.

The following articles should be brought along with you:

1. *Nourishment for 14 days (only non-perishable foods such as legumes, barley, oats, flour, canned food, etc.)*
2. *One pair of sturdy work boots, 2 pairs of socks, 2 shirts, 2 underpants, 1 work suit or dress, 2 woolen blankets, 2 sets of bed linen, a food bowl, a drinking cup, 1 spoon, 1 pullover.*
3. *Food and clothing cards, identity card and other identifying documents.*

In all other matters, you must follow unconditionally the instructions of the representatives of the Association of the Jews of Belgium.

It is explicitly forbidden to lodge a complaint against this order with any German or Belgian authority or individual. Possible objections can be presented at the assembly camp. If you fail to report to the assembly camp at the prescribed time, this will result in your capture and deportation to a concentration camp in Germany and the confiscation of all your assets.

This order should be submitted at the entrance to the assembly camp.

It was signed by SS officer Ernst Ehlers. The SS had issued more than 12,000 summonses in the hopes of assembling 300 people a day. The strategy proved an immediate failure. Less than 4,000 of the 12,000 Jews obeyed. Since most of them were recent immigrants from Germany and Eastern Europe, the past decade had taught them to be mistrustful of official Nazi appeals.

Survivor Dawid Liberman testified after the war: "All young Jews of modest means, aged 15 to 50, were to 'voluntarily' report for work.

Since they were all naive and gullible, thousands of Jews answered this call, wanting to protect their families from trouble. Three days later, information that youth was [sic] assembled in Malines with no knowledge of where they were going to be transported spread, so the rest of the young Jews who did not sign up became distrustful, and no one else applied for 'voluntary work.' Everyone was looking for a place to hide."

Two days after Malines opened, the first Jews arrived. It took five days to assemble 831 Jewish "workers". The Nazis weren't going to send a transport to the East unless it was deemed cost effective; they were shooting for 1,000 Jews. Therefore, the detainees had to endure almost a week in the camp under the authority of SS Commandant Philipp Schmitt until more Jews could be arrested. Schmitt was a brutal man who delighted in exhibiting extreme cruelty, especially when he used his prized German shepherd, Lump, to torture his prisoners. Detainee Rosy Mandel recalled in her memoir, *Holocaust Memories of Rosy Mandel*: "The worst of all Schmitt's games was the dog run. The Germans would pick one young man... and make him strip naked and run down to the courtyard. It was winter on this night and there were three or ten centimeters of snow on the ground. The Commandant watched the poor boy with hatred in his eyes. Then when the young man was tiring and becoming frozen by the weather and weak from running, Schmitt kneeled and winked at the German shepherd. The dog ran after the young Jew and attacked his scrotum and ripped out his testicles. Many times the sad note was that the victims of the dog run did not die. This... was due to freezing conditions. Their blood would coagulate and the young Jew would not bleed to death but suffer not only the physical attack and injury but also the additional humiliation of having lost his manhood. This is the kind of sadistic man Commandant Schmitt was and the horror we had to endure at Dossinkazerne..."

Since Malines was an assembly camp, only a few of the inmates were put to work. Instead, the men, women, and children were locked inside crowded rooms while the Nazis worked to fill their quota. Dozens of SS and Sipo-SD functionaries, using trucks and cars, began to methodically hunt down the Jews in Belgium. After noting the failure of the summonses to work, the Nazis organized large-scale roundups, which began on August 15, 1942. The streets were under inspection during the night; every road was shut. The Sipo-SD and its helpers burst into homes, searching from the cellars to the attics. Jews were brutally beaten and thrown, recalled Rosy Mandel: "Young and old, big and small, men, women, and children – they were all pushed into vehicles. The sick were dragged out of their beds; cripples missing one or both legs were thrown into the front of the cars. Severely ill or dying patients were taken from hospitals and sanatoriums, sent to Malines under the order for them to carry out 'voluntary' work. All of these people were selected from all over Belgium and Northern France and gathered in the barracks."

The Nazis began the first deportation procedures soon after midnight on August 4, 1942. The Jews of Malines' Transport I were lined up according to their registration numbers and put on third-class passenger trains bound for Auschwitz-Birkenau. Among them were five 61-year-olds and 51 children under the age of 15. Heartbreakingly, six children were arrested alone and deported without the comfort of their parents. None of the deportees had a clue as to where they were headed. To deter escape attempts, 25 SS guards armed with machine guns were positioned on the tops of the coaches, their muzzles pointed at the Jews as they were crammed into the trains. Yet, one 16-year-old girl, Hanna Karpowitz, managed to jump from her car while the train was still within Belgium's borders. Unfortunately, she was recaptured that same day, brought back to Malines, and placed on the next transport. She did not survive the war.

Transport I reached Auschwitz on August 5. The bewildered passengers exited the train at the *Judenrampe* [Jews' platform] located in open country halfway between Auschwitz I and Birkenau.

The Nazis murdered 25,5 percent of the deportees immediately upon arrival in one of two provisional gas chambers in Birkenau. (Larger, more efficient chambers were under construction.) The surviving Jews, 426 men and 318 women were registered and put to work in the concentration camp complex. They were subsequently decimated – ravaged by typhoid, malnutrition, exhaustion, and physical and mental abuse. Only eight people from Transport I survived the Holocaust.

From the first transport through Transport XIX, on January 15, 1943, Jews were deported in ordinary third-class passenger trains. But as greater numbers of Jews attempted to escape, the trains were replaced by windowless goods wagons. Packed in so tightly that there was no room to even sit, deportees withstood intense heat during the summer and freezing temperatures in the winter. Aside from a single bucket, there were no sanitary facilities. Through only one small vent could fresh air circulate; it was thick with the stench of urine, excrement, sweat, and vomit. Lacking food and water, many people died before they reached Auschwitz.

The armed SS guards on the convoys had orders to shoot anyone who tried to escape. One survivor, Simon Gronowski, was transported from Malines when he was only 11 years old. He recalled being packed like a herd of cattle in the train with only one bucket for 50 people to relieve themselves. How could they use it? How could they empty it? But that didn't matter, because the train was so full that it would have been impossible to get to it. There was no food, no drink, and no seating. People either sat or lay down on the floor.

As the Nazis were preparing to deport Maline's first group of prisoners that August, the Belgian-Dutch language underground newspaper, *De Vrijschutter* [The Free Shooter] reported: "[Jews] are being killed in groups by gas, and others are killed by salvos of machine gun fire." It became harder for the country's Jews to reassure themselves that the Nazis' claims of resettlement for labor purposes were the truth.

Kaserne is the German word for barracks.

13

TRANSPORT II

It took eight days for the Nazis to reach their quota for Transport II, with 839 "workers" reporting to Malines as ordered. Among them were my first cousins, Albert/Abraham and Sarah/Sura. Albert was 18; Sarah/Sura was 16. To reach the desired 1,000 deportees, the SS once more augmented the number by making arrests.

Upon arrival at Malines, each prisoner passed through the reception office, which was staffed with about a dozen Jewish women who themselves were prisoners; they'd been snatched off a train only weeks before during a raid on July 22. They had spent five days in Breendonk, a nearby Nazi prison camp, before being transferred to the assembly camp. There, these young women were appointed to act as camp secretaries. Survivor Joseph Hakker, who escaped from Transport XVIII, published a detailed testimony in 1944 about his experiences in Malines. He wrote: "[In] the registration office a voice gave the order to put everything we had into a hat...We could not keep anything. The walls were full of posters prompting us to hand in any gold, cash, diamonds, leather objects, furs, pens, food... At the first table we had to give our name, profession, address. At the second table we were registered. At the third table we had to hand over any identity papers in our possession."

If the Jews owned any property, they were forced to relinquish the keys and sign a declaration transferring ownership to the German Reich. In exchange they received a card with their transport number, which they were ordered to wear around their necks.

After registration came a physical examination. The detainees were ordered to strip. This often escalated to violence for the men and sexual assault for the women. To further humiliate them, the SS men forced women and men to disrobe in front of each other while they watched with pleasure. One female victim recalled: "I had to remove every stitch of clothing from my body. Boden (Max Boden, an SS official who often acted as a stand-in commandant when Schmitt was absent) forced me to bend over before 'searching' me. I had to remain standing with both of my feet on the ground. Boden hadn't said why I had to remove my clothes. I could only imagine that it was because he thought that I had hidden something either in my rectum or in my vagina. Boden appeared to have a great deal of pleasure... His face beamed. I had to turn round and bend over."

Survivor Valentyna Zaslawsky described the abuses a new internee could expect. "I tried to hide a small ring of little value, a memento of my brother who had died the day before my arrest. I didn't know that we were going to be searched so thoroughly that we would have to appear completely naked in front of these monsters whom I hated with all my heart. I hid the item well, but it was discovered anyway. [The SS officer] gave me a murderous look, and then jumped at me and started hitting me. My mother instinctively stood in front of me and she got hit for that twice in the face. I realized that *Les Boches* [derogatory term for Germans used during World War I, from the French word *Caboche*, meaning Cabbagehead], were disgusting brutes, and that we were doomed." Joseph Hakker wrote: "The most odious thing I witnessed was that all the photos of spouses, children,

mothers, fathers were destroyed, also letters, certificates, passports –
any belongs that had great personal value."

While Albert, Sarah, and the rest of the Jews were registered, the
suitcases they'd been ordered to leave in the courtyard were being
looted. The Nazis confiscated valuables such as knives, razors,
jewelry, money, cigarettes, and food. Items they identified as useless,
such as clothes, shoes, towels, and handkerchiefs, remained in the
suitcases, which were returned to their owners.

From the inception of the assembly camp until the end of October
1942, Belgium's Jews were plentiful enough for the Nazis to easily
fill the trains for 17 transports. In August alone, six full transports left
the camp. Five departed in September. The following month, three
double transports were sent to Auschwitz-Birkenau. Therefore,
Albert and Sarah only had to endure a few days in the camp. In the
next two years, however, the numbers of transports dwindled as more
and more Jews went into hiding. In 1943, there were only six, and
only five in 1944. After 1942, because it was taking the Nazis longer
and longer to collect the desired 1,000 Jews per transport, some
detainees spent months in Malines.

On August 11, 1942, my cousins left for Poland on Transport II, two
young people among 1,000 Jews: 484 men, 516 women. Fifty-one of
them were children under the age of 15. The youngest was five-year-
old Benito Braystayn; Dora Lustig was the oldest, at 63-years-old.

Albert and Sarah arrived at Auschwitz in the early morning, the
train's breaks squealing to a halt at the Judenrampe. The doors to all
the wagons were opened; the Jews blinked at the sudden intrusion of
light. SS men armed with machine guns and growling dogs on
straining leashes greeted them. They barked orders to the stunned
passengers.

"*Raus! Alles raus verfluchte Hunde!*" [Get out! Everyone out, you
goddamned dogs!]

Albert and Sarah did not survive to leave testimony of their suffering. But Dennis Urstein, who arrived to the death camp from Malines just 16 days later did.

"There was screaming and shouting. We... saw people that were running around in striped uniforms. A lot of SS with dogs, with rifles and pistols. We lined up, women to the left with the children and all men to the right. And then we went through the routine of the selection where the physician – I shouldn't use that word because he was just a butcher – was standing there. And when I came up he asked me, 'What is your profession?' 'I'm a tailor,' [I answered.] 'Go.' He pointed to the right. And we marched into Auschwitz. The first thing I saw was the sign, *Arbeit Macht Frei* [Work will set you free]. I saw a bunch of block buildings. They weren't barracks. This was Auschwitz I, the main camp. [Then] I saw a sight that stays with me until today. It was early in the morning. I saw some characters that looked extremely healthy, very muscular. They were Russian soldiers. There weren't too many because they killed all the Russian soldiers and kept the minimum. And [I saw] some Polish speaking and Ukrainian speaking guys that pushed a cart. They stopped in front of [us] and all of a sudden bodies came shooting out. Later on I learned that they were called the Harvester *Kommando* [work squad]. They were the people that picked up the bodies that either were killed during the night or died during the night. And they picked them up and took them to an assembly place where later on they were picked up on a truck and brought to a crematorium."

Dawid Liberman, who arrived from Malines on October 26, 1942, recalled the emotional torture. "Scenes of atrocity accompanied the separation of families." When loved ones balked at being parted from one another, the guards used their whips, truncheons, and dogs to great effectiveness.

Mr. Liberman, although on a different transport from Mr. Urstein, recounted an arrival to Auschwitz that was nearly identical. "The SS men came to supervise the men," recalled Liberman. "They would point with their thumb, sending people left and right in order to separate the young and healthy prisoners from the weak and elderly. The same thing happened to women and children. Young and healthy women were on one side, weak and old on the other. A searchlight was turned on. In its swath of light appeared a Nazi officer in a dark green uniform. He climbed onto a small platform as each line of bewildered deportees slowly began to move forward. When each person passed in front of the platform, the officer scrutinized them, then waved his riding crop to the left or to the right. Those bunched on the left were the middle-aged or older, the frail, and the children."

No doubt, my cousins Albert and Sarah were subjected to scenes much like the ones recounted by Liberman and Urstein.

From Transport II, 292 men and 228 women were selected for labor. The remaining 481 – the condemned – were marched towards a white, windowless building sitting innocuously beside a small forest. Primitive wooden barracks had been erected nearby. They were told that they were being sent to the camp, but first they had to bathe and undergo disinfection. Guards directed them to the barracks to disrobe. With the Final Solution still in its infancy, it is doubtful that any rumors of Jews being gassed had reached them. They complied. Once everyone was naked, they were herded inside the white building. The doors were shut and locked behind them. The pretense was over. An SS man wearing a gas mask deposited the blue Zyklon-B pellets into a small opening in the roof. The pellets instantly transformed into poisonous gas, taking only six to seven minutes to extinguish hundreds of lives. Once the SS were sure that everyone was dead, the doors were opened to ventilate the building. Members of the *Sonderkommando* [special squad] charged with the disposal of gas chamber victims, got to work. First they extricated the twisted and intertwined corpses before removing them. Then they scrubbed the little white house clean of the urine, excrement, and vomit that had been eliminated in the victims' final moments. Prison dentists pulled gold teeth out of mouths; prison barbers cut long hair from the dead women and girls. Then all the bodies were carried to the nearby ditch that had been sprinkled with lime in anticipation of their arrival. The bodies were thrown in and torched. When the incineration was complete, the ashes were either buried or thrown into the nearby Vistula River. It was as if 1,000 people had never existed.[1]

The men and women of Transport II chosen for labor, having passed their first *Selektion* – but not their last – were tattooed with their registration numbers and admitted to the camp. There was an average of four deaths a day among the laborers of Transport II.

The Nazis were meticulous recordkeepers. There are approximately 30 million pages of surviving records. But there are no Auschwitz records for Albert or Sarah. They both fell within the age limit to be chosen for labor, and perhaps they were. But the statistics don't favor that. The circumstances, the moment, and the place of their death is not known. I hope they died together. I hope they had each other to cling to as their young lives, full of promise, were snuffed out.

The first gas chamber at Auschwitz was in the main camp, Auschwitz I, and was constructed by SS engineers in the basement of the prison block, Block 11. Later, a larger, permanent gas chamber – the Crematorium I – was constructed in a separate building outside the prisoner compound. It had been adapted to kill several hundred people at a time. As the Nazis beefed up their extermination program, a second gas chamber went into operation in the spring of 1942 in a specially adapted farmhouse, the Nazis having ejected the family that lived there. Called the "Red House" (aka Bunker I), it stood outside the fence of Birkenau, which was still under construction. The windows of the house were walled up and the interior reconfigured; two barracks were erected nearby. When the

45

chamber was ready, it had the capacity to gas 800 people at once, but 800 was found to be insufficient. Another family was dislodged in mid-1942 and their house, also located just outside the Birkenau camp fence, was adapted into another gas chamber, called Bunker II or the "White House," with the capacity to kill 1,200 people at a time. Three barracks for undressing were erected nearby. This second chamber is where Albert and Sarah were most likely gassed.

For my cousins to survive the war, they would have had to suffer over three years in a camp system designed to kill, if not outright, then through unendurable labor, starvation rations, and improper clothing. Labor performed indoors, such as in the kitchen or the sauna (laundry disinfection building), allowed for a better chance of survival than heavy labor conducted outdoors. So did having a useful skill, occupation, or talent. Carpenters and masons were favored, as the camp was in a constant state of expansion. Medical practitioners were utilized in the camp "hospital" where, in reality, the only medicine practiced was sadistic experimentation. Singers and piano players entertained the Nazis as they sipped their schnapps during after-hours parties, and musicians performed in the camp orchestra, forced to serenade slave workers as they departed to their Kommandos and returned at night.

---

1. To ensure that the killings were carried out with the greatest secrecy, the SS kept the Sonderkommando prisoners isolated from the rest of the camp population and routinely killed them after a short time on the job. As eyewitnesses to the worst atrocities, they were too dangerous to survive.

14

JEAN-PIERRE

While my parents were busy with their resistance work, I was in the loving care of my war parents. Gerard and Germaine made the decision to raise me dressed as a girl since I was circumcised, as is customary for Jewish boys. It was doubtful that even the most hardened Nazi would ask a little girl to pull down her pants for religious identification. Until the end of the war, I wore dresses and bows in my hair. The Decraenes never addressed me as Jean-Pierre, opting instead for pet names such as *Pouyou*, a French-language Belgian term of endearment, and *Pierette*. I never had a haircut, and my beribboned, thick ringlets made me look very feminine, and, I have to admit, pretty.

Aside from being Jewish, my parents hid me with the Decraenes because they risked being arrested if they were caught performing resistance activities. They weren't aware that Germaine and Gerard, who spoke perfect German, were involved in anti-German activities far more deeply than themselves. Gerard was a double agent. On behalf of the British, Gerard and Germaine pretended to be Nazi sympathizers, regularly hosting evening soirees for the SS in their parlor while plying them with alcohol. If their guests began spilling war secrets (and they often did, as they loved to brag about their achievements) Gerard would go down to the basement late at night and tap all the useful intelligence in Morse code into a transmitter hidden in the coal bin. The messages went directly to England. Some of the secrets he extracted detailed the location of reinforcements on Belgium's beaches, where the Nazis had built bunkers and emplacements. Gerard also obtained blueprints, which were successfully smuggled to the U.K.

Once, a secret he obtained inadvertently made the Nazi from whom he procured it very happy. During one cocktail party, this particular officer was complaining about how he hated his boss. He divulged to Gerard that the boss had a mistress, the name of the restaurant the man frequented, and more information about his daily routine. Gerard forwarded the intelligence to his handlers and the man was killed by the Resistance. The next time Gerard saw the Nazi, the man shared how happy he was about his boss's demise.

Another scoop of Gerard's concerned the location of a secret *Abwehr* [German military intelligence service] base in the woods near a town called Keerbergen, about 35 kilometers from Brussels. Based on Gerard's work, the British bombed it to bits. (When I was about eight, Gerard took me there to pick mushrooms and I saw the ruined buildings and underground bunkers.)

My parents had no idea that I was an adorable attendee of these parties, regularly bounced on the knees of the very people who wanted to kill me. But bounce me they did, delighting in my squeals of pleasure. One officer even brought me a wooden toy, which was a real treat because I didn't have many playthings at the time. Gerard even attended Nazi meetings with other Belgian sympathizers to further ingratiate himself into the Nazis' trust.

My parents came to see me when they felt it was safe. I have photographs from some of those visits. The last one was taken when I was about 18 months old, in the late summer or early fall of 1942.

Only my mother is in the photograph with me. Shortly after this, a female neighbor a few doors down from the Decraenes became romantically involved with a member of the Gestapo, the brutal Nazi Internal Security organization. Gerard and Germaine were uneasy about her new relationship, afraid she would denounce them to the Nazis due to Germaine's instantaneous motherhood. Being denounced would mean certain death for all of us, including my parents. They decided to move me back to the farm. Even there, I maintained my female identity. Gerard and Germaine visited every weekend after I went to live there.

The farm in Vilvoorde was in the Flemish-speaking part of Belgium, and Flemish was spoken in the home, although Gerard's mother, whom I called Bomma, also spoke French. Since I was just learning how to speak, I became completely bilingual.

I loved life on the farm. I had other children to play with for the first time in my life. Living nearby were my war cousins Simone and Jacqueline, the daughters of Gerard's sister and brother. Another benefit of living on the farm was that there was plenty to eat. There was very little milk or cheese, and sugar was rationed, but there were plenty of vegetables, lettuces, potatoes, and rabbits. There were apple and cherry trees and a strawberry patch, as well as goats, sheep, and a donkey that I loved to ride. As I got older, I was allowed to help at harvesting time. When it was time to dig up the potatoes, I would collect dead leaves for a bonfire. When the flames were ready, Bomma would put the freshly dug potatoes into the fire. For supper, we'd feast on them with freshly churned goat and sheep butter. War seemed very far away at the farm.

15

A ROYAL INTERVENTION

On August 1, 1942, Queen Mother Elisabeth of Belgium, the mother of King Leopold III, met with representatives of the AJB in her royal palace in Brussels. They told her about the atrocities being committed in Belgium, as well as the imprisonment conditions in Malines. The Queen Mother promised her visitors that she would do everything in her power to stop the arrests and to protect the Belgian Jews from being deported. Only six percent of the Jewish population held Belgian passports. She made no such promises pertaining to the Jews without Belgian citizenship. Restricting protection to Belgian nationals implied that the rest of the country's Jews could be abandoned.

Via the Italian royal family and the Red Cross, Queen Mother Elisabeth turned directly to Hitler to request that Belgian Jews not be deported. In a telegram from Berlin, she was promised that those currently under arrest in Malines awaiting deportation could receive visitors, and that Jews with Belgian citizenship would not be deported or separated from their families. The Queen Mother was a pawn used by the Sipo-SD in the latter promise, for which they had a motive: to keep families together so that later they could deport whole families – the young children and the elderly – in their entirety. The German response was forwarded to representatives of the AJB. The Queen Mother's secretary brought to the AJB's attention that they were only talking about a promise, and that the Queen Mother would continue to follow the fate of her Jewish subjects.

Less than three months later, the Nazis arrested the children in the AJB-sponsored Wezembeek orphanage, a home for those whose parents had already been deported. After Queen Mother Elisabeth pushed the Germans on this issue, the children were released. In June 1943, the Queen Mother protested once again regarding the Belgian Jews imprisoned in Malines, and about 300 of them were immediately released. Queen Elisabeth also intervened in a number of individual cases.

The Nazis did not keep their promises, though. Most of the Jews with Belgian nationality were rounded up and arrested in one swoop on September 3, 1943. Seventeen days later, they were deported to Auschwitz on Transport XXII. Despite the meager results, and the fact that the Queen-Mother's intervention related to a limited number of Jews, the actions on behalf of the Jews by a member of the royal family in Europe was unparalleled throughout the rest of the continent.

16

TRANSPORT XX

Israel Rosengarten was a 16-year-old Polish-born former high school student from Antwerp when he was deported on Transport VIII. He recalled after the war, "In the early transports the trains were routed through small, out-of-the-way stations which meant it would have taken several hours to cross into Germany." He described the surreal quality of being in enemy territory. While the SS guards were allowed to get off the train for a coffee or a glass of beer, as if it were a normal journey, Rosengarten testified: "We were cut off from everything. People glanced at us from time to time, but there was no one who seemed to care about what was going on. Our suffering was for us alone. Nobody would help us." But he was wrong.

On April 19, 1943, Transport XX departed Malines at approximately 10:15 p.m. carrying 1,631 Jews in 30 cars. It was the first transport from the camp to use cattle cars. The convoy had not progressed very far when it was stopped by a man on the track waving a red lamp, Youra Livschitz, a Russian-born Jewish medical student who had been active in the Resistance since 1942. After a group of Jewish resistance members were arrested and sent to Malines, Livschitz devised a plan to intercept a train and free as many people as possible. The Underground was skeptical but Livschitz was undeterred. He recruited two non-Jewish school friends from his pre-medical school days, Jean Franklemon and Robert Maistriau. Very quickly, the three men worked out their rudimentary plan: to signal the engineer to stop the train by using red paper to cover the glass of a lantern. Their only supplies were a single pistol and some pliers. It worked.

When the engineer saw the red light, it signified danger ahead; he immediately hit the brakes. When the train came to a stop, Livschhitz held him at gunpoint while Franklemon and Maistriau cut the locks on one of the car doors. Maistriau later recalled: "The brakes made a hellish noise and at first I was petrified. But then I gave myself a jolt on the basis that if you have started something you should go through with it. I held my torch in my left hand and with my right, I had to busy myself with the pliers. I was very excited and it took far too long until I had cut through the wire that secured the bolts of the sliding door. I shone my torch into the carriage and pale and frightened faces stared back at me. I shouted: 'Sortez Sortez!' [French for 'Get out! Get out!'] and then, 'Schnell Schnell, fliehen Sie!' [German for 'Please hurry!']."

Seventeen Jews escaped from the car under heavy gunfire from the SS. Others, who had prepared for escape while detained at Malines, managed to cut holes into the sides and floors of their cars. They forced the doors open using saws, knives, iron bars, and pliers that had been furnished to them by several sympathetic electricians, carpenters, and plumbers employed throughout Malines. Unbeknownst to Livschitz, Franklemon, and Maistriau, there were several former escapees on Transport XX, as well, who were on their second trip to Auschwitz. They lost none of their nerve in attempting to escape again.

By the time the train reached the German border, 236 deportees had fled, some of them wounded in the process. From this group, 26 were shot or received fatal injuries when they jumped, 80-90 were recaptured, and 120 succeeded in escaping. Seventeen of them were from the car Maistriau freed. Many who escaped found refuge in Belgian homes.

Transport XX was the *only* instance during World War II when a Nazi transport carrying Jews was stopped. As punishment for the attack, and to deter future deportees from attempting to escape, the Nazis gassed all the Jews in every other wagon of Transport XX upon arrival at Auschwitz, regardless of their fitness for labor.

Robert Maistriau continued working with the Resistance but was captured in 1944, deported to Buchenwald, and liberated by the Americans. Jean Franklemon was sent to a concentration camp. He survived the war. Youra Livschitz was caught months after the attack and executed as a "communist terrorist," bravely refusing to wear a blindfold as he faced the firing squad.

17

CAREFREE DAYS ON THE FARM

Soon after I went to live on the farm, we celebrated Saint Nicholas Day. In Belgium, children believe that Saint Nicholas brings presents on December 5 (Saint Nicholas Eve) and on December 6 (Saint Nicholas Day). Children put their shoes in front of the fireplace along with a gift for Saint Nicholas, such as a drawing or cookies. They might also leave a carrot for Saint Nicholas's horse. Then Saint Nicholas arrives on the roof, climbs down the chimney, and leaves presents in and around the shoes. Christmas is recognized on December 25, but it is more of a religious occasion.

Every Christmas we feasted on lavish meals such as chicken roasted in the oven with lots of butter, mussels, French fries, rabbit in mustard sauce, goose, duck, white asparagus, and endive with cheese sauce. It was a memorable time and I can recall glimpses of Christmas time in December 1943 when I was just shy of my third birthday. I was as eager as any other child in Belgium, anticipating the goodies that Saint Nicholas would bring me and the foods we would eat.

18

AUNT CELINA AND UNCLE FISZEL ARE ARRESTED

On October 26, 1943, Celina and Fiszel were arrested by the Sipo-SD at Kaytan. Presumably my father was also employed at the store, but he was not arrested that day. Perhaps he wasn't there when the Nazis showed up.

By the spring of 1943, most of Belgium's Jews had gone into hiding. Therefore, the Nazis abstained from mass raids since they were largely unfruitful. Instead, they relied on special arresting squads consisting of the SD (the local Security Service of the SS), detectives sent from Berlin, the Flemish SS from Antwerp, and the *Feldgendarmerie* [German Military Police]. A host of collaborators were also recruited to hunt Jews: bounty hunters who, until 1944, received payment for each Jew they denounced. Even so, the SD found it difficult to provide a constant flow of Jews into Malines. The number of daily arrests from the fall of 1942 to the spring of 1944 continued to decline. It took the Nazis nearly four months to complete the deportation list for Transport XVIII. They had been trying to fill it since September 22, 1943. My move to the farm coincided with the arrests of Celina and Fiszel, and may have contributed to it.

My aunt and uncle spent over two months in Malines, but at least the sadistic Commandant Phillip Schmitt had been replaced by Johannes Frank, a man who didn't share in his predecessor's brutality, though there remained plenty of guards who did.

Frank had been assigned to temporarily fill in for Schmitt when the latter took a vacation in March 1943. During this period, Frank discovered that Schmitt was involved in black market activities, profiting from the sale of leather goods and other products made by skilled prisoners – goods that were supposed to profit the Reich. Frank reported Schmitt to the authorities and became his replacement. He attempted to improve conditions for the prisoners with a better food supply and a reduction of abuses. For example, the physical exam of the women was administered henceforth by a Jewish prisoner or a sister of an SS officer rather than by a male SS officer.

A typical day for a prisoner in Malines went as follows: After sleeping in unheated rooms on filthy straw mattresses without blankets, up to 120 prisoners per room were woken up at 6 a.m. with a shout of "*Aufstehen!*" [Get up!] There was only one washroom for men and one for women. To humiliate all the prisoners, the women had to pass through the men's washroom, with its urinals in full view, to get to their washroom.

Next came the first roll call of the day. Recalled Rosy Mandel, "If no one was missing or had died during the night, roll call went smoothly; if there was a problem, it could take hours, and if that happened we might miss breakfast."[1]

Breakfast was 225 grams of bread and three-quarters of a liter of black water, euphemistically called coffee. Two times a week, the prisoners were only given 112 grams of bread. The evening meal consisted of three-quarters of a liter of watery cabbage soup and half a spoon of honey or sugar.

The prisoners were locked in their quarters for 22 hours a day. Only two hours per day were spent outside: one for another roll call at 2:30 p.m. and one for an hour of walking in the courtyard. The lack of exercise and fresh air combined with the poor quality and quantity of food and increasingly longer stays in Malines led to new problems: overpopulation and epidemic diseases like scabies and impetigo. Sanitary conditions also deteriorated since clothing was seldom laundered. People wore the same undergarments for months, creating the perfect breeding ground for lice.

There were physical abuses, as well. Prisoner Joseph Hakker recounted a favorite pastime of the guards during his captivity, a practice which they continued with subsequent groups. "One of the inspections – the most detested by the prisoners and the most favorite of the *gaolers* [jailers] – was the examination of the feet. Neither body nor limbs were examined: only the soles of the feet. This control would not have been so disagreeable, if only the gentlemen had not done it, as was generally the case, at the dead of night after having drunk heavily in their casino. We could regularly expect two of these foot-controls a week. The orderly was held responsible for the corporal cleanliness of his men. In the course of three months, I got only twice an opportunity of taking a shower-bath of ten minutes, including undressing and dressing. Some old people never got an opportunity. We had to wash ourselves with cold water in an unheated room, usually without soap. Rather young men, who formerly went in for sports, could pull it off. For hundreds of women and children it was a torture. Some persons were in such a condition of foulness that we preferred to fight shy of them on account of the fume. But the soles of the feet had to be clean, most likely not to dirty the reeking mattresses which we had to sleep on. The gentlemen decided to control the feet at Christmas during the night of 25 to 26 December. At about 2 a.m., a light was brought in and the orderly was called; he had to rise immediately and to put on his shoes but got no time to dress properly. He had to come to attention in pajamas and say:

'Mr. Lieutenant (the Germans always add the rank when addressing an officer) – the orderly of room___ is present. The room is occupied by___ persons.' The lieutenant, who always carries his chip, and the non-commissioned officer begin to shout: 'Feet bare!' They slap the beds with the whip, and men, women and children must show their feet. And woe to the unfortunate creatures whose feet are not deemed clean enough! Barefooted they must go to the wash-place, right across the vast square. This night our herculean lieutenant was drunk, everybody saw him stagger. One of the women in our room had to go downstairs barefooted, together with 22 from other rooms, and walk in the snow for 20 minutes, and [wearing only] night dress."

Survivor Chaja Rifka Rozenszayn-Leizerowicz, detained with Celina and Fiszel also attested to the middle-of-the-night cleanliness checks. She added that if even one person's feet were judged filthy, everybody endured a foot flogging administered with a leather strap.

---

1. At its peak, Malines held more than 2,000 people at a time.

19

TRANSPORT XXIII

Although there were constant rumors circulating the camp, the prisoners were given no notice of their deportation. Rosy Mandel wrote: "Did anyone talk about Auschwitz in Malines? Yes, but discreetly, there might have been spies. But prisoners talked about it. A lot of people knew about it, a lot didn't, and a lot didn't want to know."

On the morning of January 15, 1944, Celina and Fiszel were woken at 3 a.m. and told to prepare themselves to be taken by truck to the Malines rail station. They each received a loaf of bread to sustain them on the 1,200-kilometer journey.

Transport XXIII was the first deportation from Malines in 1944 and contained a considerably lower number of deportees than the previous transports. Each cattle car was loaded with about 50 people and one latrine bucket. In the freezing January cold, the Jews of Transport XXIII had to endure six hours in the cars before the wheels began to turn. Once the train was moving, and before crossing the border into Germany, five passengers tried to escape. One of them, 35-year-old Chaja Freedman-Cukier, had previously escaped from

Transport XX. She would be given no more opportunities. For this attempt she was shot.

Suffering two days of extreme cold and deprivation, several passengers fell ill and died before they reached Auschwitz. Upon arrival, 416 people were found unfit for work and immediately gassed. The Nazis selected 238 for forced labor: 140 men and 98 women, including Aunt Celina. Since there is no record for Uncle Fiszel, I assume he was dispatched to one of four sophisticated new crematoriums containing gas chambers with a capacity to kill 2,000 at a time and burn over 4,000 corpses a day.

The newcomers were greeted by the Sonderkommandos working a 12-hour shift. Twenty of them in the undressing room gave the Fiszel and the others instructions to fold and pile their clothes neatly, and to remember where they had placed them so they could retrieve them after their "shower." Within 20 minutes, the gas would have killed them all.

Ten members of the Sonderkommando were tasked with cleaning the gas chamber. Six harvested dental gold. Another six loaded the corpses onto a hoist that connected the basement to the ground floor. Eight men maintained the oven fires and loaded the furnaces. By the day's end, just like his children Albert and Sarah, every trace of Fiszel Wajs was gone.

20

CELINA IN BIRKENAU

Having passed the inaugural Selektion, Celina was led to the entrance of Auschwitz I and marched through the gate under its infamous sign. She was tattooed and recorded as a prisoner before being sent to Birkenau. Her initiation occurred in the bathhouse, where she and the other women from Transport XXIII were lined up in the corridor. Two female prisoners and three male SS guards brought five prisoners at a time into a nearby room. When Celina was led in, she was ordered to undress quickly and put her clothes and underwear aside. When one of the women balked at disrobing in front of the male guards, her complaint was answered with a rubber truncheon to her back. Celina obediently shed her clothes as quickly as she could and submitted to having all the hair on her head and body shaved, trying not to wince as the rough blade nicked her skin. She thought of Albert and especially young Sarah and wondered if they too had endured such humiliations. Completely naked, she was rushed into the bathhouse in front of the men from her transport. At the entrance stood a female prisoner holding a sprayer which she used to delouse the prisoners. The liquid burned Celina in all the places where her skin had been cut by the razor.

After delousing, the women were driven by beatings into a steam room where they stayed for over an hour. Then, straight from the heat, they were chased into another room to receive the ubiquitous striped uniforms: either a dress or a skirt, a jacket, and a headscarf. No regards were given to their sizes. Heavy women received uniforms that they couldn't stretch over their frames, while small women received ones that swam on them. The "hygiene" procedures recently forced upon them made no sense. The uniforms were dirty, torn, damp, and ironically, covered with lice. Instead of shoes, they were given primitive wooden or leather clogs with canvas tops. No socks were distributed.

The day's final indignity came next. Under supervision of the SS, 20 female prisoners tasked with filling out forms with prisoners' personal data sat in a room connected to the bathhouse. Prisoners from each transport were organized in alphabetical order. Then their surname, given name, and nationality were written down in a *Nummerbuch* [Book of Numbers]. Celina was stripped of her pretty French name. She was now 74605, and if she ever forgot it, all she had to do was look at the new tattoo on her forearm.

21

TRANSPORT XXIV

Rosa and Charles were sick with worry when Celina and Fiszel were arrested. Albert and Sarah had been gone for over two years and never heard from again. It was hard not to dwell on the unthinkable. My parents could have given up their resistance activities, but instead Celina and Fiszel's expulsion from Belgium reasserted their faith that their anti-Nazi work must continue.

The railroad tracks outside Malines were quiet for the rest of January, February, and March. The Nazis were having difficulties rounding up enough Jews to justify the expense of a transport. Most of Belgium's Jews were in hiding or had already been sent east. Nevertheless, a new transport was formed. It took 84 days to compile the list – much longer than for earlier transports. Jews who had stayed in the assembly camp for an extended period, perhaps because they were performing a useful labor, were now added to the list.

They had been able to hold out for so long, but the Nazis finally caught up with them. On an unknown date between January and the earliest days of April 1944, my parents were arrested. My mother claimed that she had been working alone on the streets distributing anti-Nazi leaflets when she was apprehended by the Nazis. She told me that after she was arrested, she never saw my father again. But records show that my parents were arrested together and sent to Malines on the same transport. I have no idea how much time they endured at the assembly camp, but my safety must have given them a measure of comfort.

At 4 a.m. on April 4, 1944, the wagons for Transport XXIV arrived on the tracks at Malines. When my mother spoke of Auschwitz, she claimed she had never heard of the camp or of any rumors of Nazis burning Jews. I don't think she was being truthful. So late in the war, how could she have possibly been deaf to the stories and rumors?

There were 626 deportees in my parents' transport: 14 Jews who had been in Malines as early as 1942; 92 Jews there since 1943; 520 who had trickled in one by one or in small groups; and 20 who had escaped from earlier transports and been recaptured. The escapees, whose names were given special notations on the transport lists, were assigned to a special wagon that was to be scrupulously guarded.

For each wagon, the Nazis assigned one Jew to be responsible for the entire group. They threatened dire consequences to this unfortunate individual if anyone was missing on arrival – dead or alive. This meant that whoever wanted to try and escape first had to persuade the wagon foreman to flee as well. If the foreman refused, a fight would likely follow. Only after the foreman was overpowered would it be possible to file through the tiny window and bend through the bars. The opening had to be sufficiently enlarged for a body to get through. Often those about to escape preferred sawing through the floorboards and slipping out between the train and the track through the bottom of the car. One needed great courage to choose such a dangerous method of escape. But the train's destination was even more threatening.

Soon after the wagons arrived on the tracks, the prisoners had to line up in the courtyard in order according to their registration number.

My father was 234, my mother was 235, proof that her statement about never seeing my father again was untrue.

The journey was abominable, the stench insufferable. As with every other journey to the camps, there was one bucket of drinkable water in each overstuffed car, and one latrine bucket that quickly overflowed onto the straw-strewn floor. The convoy's motion meant that the nasty swill reached all four corners of the car. Space was so limited that people had to take turns sleeping. Some people died. Rosa forced herself to remain calm by repeatedly telling herself she was going to a labor camp. Soon there was no drinking water left. The car was only opened for the guards to do escape checks. Only once was the car opened to give the passengers water. During this stop, there was a discussion about whether anyone should try to escape before the train started moving again. The group decided that the odds of surviving an attempt were too small; the convoy was riddled with armed SS guards.

As Transport XXIV proceeded toward its sinister destination, people became hysterical. Many had diarrhea, forced to relieve themselves in their undergarments. It must have become nearly impossible for my mother to believe that a labor camp could be the cause of such hysteria. Some passengers knew they were going to Auschwitz. Others, like my mother, didn't want to know.

Despite the cautionary measures taken by the SS, two men managed to jump from one of the cars. Emil Weber was recaptured, imprisoned in Aachen, Germany, and returned to Malines. Deported on the next transport, he survived the war. Ludwig Falkenstein jumped out between the German cities of Stendal and Magdeburg. He was recaptured the next day and deported to Auschwitz in May 1944. He also survived.

On April 6, 1944, Birkenau registered 36,000 prisoners, the greatest number admitted in a single day: 15,000 men and 21,000 women. My parents arrived the next day. As their train approached, the SS greeting party extinguished their cigarettes. Birkenau's well-oiled machine wound to a start – the dogs, the shouting, the brutal unloading of the stunned and exhausted Jews. They were immediately divided into groups of five-across; the men were separated from the women and children. Before my mother knew it, my father was no longer beside her. She never saw him again. This time, she was telling the truth.

As the members of Transport XXIV were being prepared for Selektion, prisoners in striped uniforms entered the cars and tossed out their belongings. These were the prisoners employed in the so-called "Kanada" commando, one of the most coveted of the Kommandos. Kanada Kommando was tasked with collecting all the property belonging to the new arrivals and bringing it to giant warehouses to be sorted, stored, and shipped back to Germany. The nickname Kanada came from the prisoners, who viewed Canada as a wealthy and resource-rich country. Throughout Auschwitz's existence, Kanada's 30 storage sheds overflowed with goods. On average, five freight cars filled with stolen belongings left Auschwitz daily.

Rosa stood in her row, watching the pile of bags growing into a veritable mountain outside the doors of the cars. She craned her neck searching fruitlessly for Charles before her turn to face the camp doctor. Finally, she was in the first row. The doctor stood imposingly in front of her.

"Age?" he asked.

"Thirty-two," she answered.

The next question shocked her: "How many gold teeth do you have?"

She was stunned into silence. She hadn't been expecting that. When she didn't answer immediately, she thought the doctor would hit her. It was beyond her imagination to think she was being appraised for her potential to enrich the Reich through her death – the death the doctor believed was inevitable.

"None," she stammered when she regained her voice.

"Children?" he countered.

Once again, his question caught her off-guard. If she admitted she had a son, he would demand to know where he was. She couldn't tell him Jean-Pierre was in hiding with a Gentile couple in Belgium.

"Children!" he demanded, impatiently.

Thinking quickly, Rosa said, "I *had* a son. " Even in a lie, she couldn't bear to say that I was deceased. But her vague implication seemed to appease the doctor. And it *was* true, in a way. She'd had a son – had given birth to one. And she didn't have me now. The doctor directed my mother to the right with a flick of his finger. He was already focusing his attention to the next woman in line.

When the Selektion was concluded, 206 men and 149 women were admitted to the camp. The other 279 were sent to the gas chambers. My father had also been chosen as a laborer, but of course my mother didn't know that.

It is incomprehensible to me how anyone could pass Selektion after a journey of three days or more with virtually no food, no water, no sleep, no room to stretch out, no opportunity to clean oneself, and having to sit or stand in the body fluids of themselves and others. As my parents marched into the camp, they got their first look at the filthy and emaciated old-timers of Birkenau.

22

CHARLES IN BIRKENAU

As Charles stood on a stool, submitting to a full-body shave, he couldn't believe how much his life had changed in such a short time. Then he received his prison uniform. He was a man who took great pride in dressing well. He had been employed by (or owned, if my mother was to be believed) a successful business selling the latest in men's fashion so that his patrons also looked their best. Now he was reduced to being a hairless prisoner clad in an infested uniform. How had his life come to this? Was it even real?

The uniforms, like every facet of existence in Birkenau, were part of the camp's killing mechanism. Of the clothing issued to the prisoners, expert witness Professor Jan Olbrycht testified on October 5, 1947 to the Investigation of German Crimes in Poland: "I have been involved in issues concerning health, hygiene, nutrition and medical care at the former Auschwitz-Birkenau concentration camp while acting as an expert witness in the case of Rudolf Höss, the camp's long-standing commandant. The clothes handed out to prisoners did not provide sufficient protection against atmospheric factors, and in particular the cold and damp. Garments were identical for inmates who worked under a roof and for those toiling outdoors, irrespective of the weather. The footwear was exceptionally substandard. The majority of inmates worked in clogs, and these caused serious abrasions of the skin. Since, as I have already mentioned, conditions in the camp were unhygienic, infections would set in leading to deep phlegmons that accounted for a large percentage of ailments requiring surgical intervention. Both bedlinen and underwear were changed infrequently and irregularly. They would be washed carelessly, so that it was not uncommon for prisoners to receive 'clean' bedlinen or underwear that was ridden with lice. These terrible hygienic conditions resulted in thousands of inmates becoming infested with lice, or contracting scabies or ringworms."

Once my father was registered, he was assigned to a quarantine block with 39 other men to prevent the spread of infectious diseases. Depending on the sizes of incoming transports, various places were set aside for quarantine: entire blocks, huts, or primitive tents. Even horse stables housed newcomers, outfitted with three-tiered wooden bunks furnished with dirty straw and filthy blankets shared among multiple people. The Nazis had no intention of letting the quarantining prisoners lay idle. Until they could join the camp population and a labor detail, the SS would begin the extermination process by devising elaborate games to exhaust the men. Being kept busy playing games may not sound like a bad way for quarantined prisoners to pass the time, especially when the alternative was backbreaking labor. The average prisoner of Birkenau had a lifespan of three weeks. But the SS were creative in mixing sport with torture. The combination of meager rations and punishingly brutal drills soon weakened the segregated men. For example, they had to perform a "dance" which consisted of spinning around in circles while holding the left foot with the left hand and simultaneously keeping the right hand stretched out and the head straight up. Failure to execute the drill correctly resulted in a beating.

The quarantine barracks were where prisoners began to see Auschwitz for what it was: a place where they were not regarded as human, where privacy was non-existent, and brutal punishment for the most arbitrary of offenses was the rule of law. It was a place devoid of medical treatment, where the diet lacked nutrition to sustain life, and where the most basic of human functions – the elimination of waste, was based on schedule rather than need. Chanan Akavia was imprisoned with my father from their time in quarantine until the last days of the war. In his postwar testimony, he aptly described the Birkenau by *not* describing it. He was, "limited by human language that could not describe the horrors of the first two days in Auschwitz."

23

SUBCAMPS

In the first years of the concentration camp system as a whole, and later, in Auschwitz, many concentration camp prisoners worked at expanding the camp infrastructure. Little thought was given to utilizing prisoner labor for the benefit of the German economy or the war effort. That changed in 1942, though, as a result of the military setbacks suffered by the Wehrmacht on the Eastern front in the winter battles of 1941 and 1942. Heavy material losses led to Hitler's decision to increase armament production. The Third Reich was also desperate for labor in coal mines, steel works, chemical plants, and other businesses to keep the war going.

On April 30, 1942, Oswald Pohl, head of the SS *Wirtschafts-und Verwaltungshauptamt* / WVHA [SS Main Economic and Administrative Office] in Berlin issued the following regulations formalizing the organization of the labor system in the concentration camps:

1. There is no limit to working hours. Their duration depends on the kind of labor establishments in the camps and the

kind of labor to be done. They are fixed by the camp commandants alone.

2. Any circumstances which may result in a shortening of working hours (e.g. meals or roll calls) and which cannot be condensed any more, have therefore to be restricted to the absolute minimum. It is forbidden to allow long walks to the place of work and noon intervals (if not for eating purposes).

Central SS authorities tried to persuade camp commandants to focus their efforts on keeping the working prisoners alive to serve the German war effort. This demonstrates the Reich's real desire and need for useful labor by the prisoners, as opposed to the weak production capabilities of starved, weakened, and abused prisoners. Few of the commandants heeded these instructions. None were concerned with changing the murderous culture of the camps, even for the benefit of the Reich.

Lacking sufficient civilian workers, private and state-owned companies were begging for forced laborers and prisoners of war. In 1943, SS Chief Heinrich Himmler complied to their request to further augment the workforce with concentration camp prisoners. So many prisoners were assigned to work for external companies that between 1942 and 1944, hundreds of subcamps were established under the commands of main concentration camps such as Auschwitz (which had almost 40), or Mauthausen (which had over 40), in or near factories or sites for extraction of raw materials.

Up until 1944, the road to Auschwitz had been a largely one-way street. In the camp's first four years, more than 800,000 deportees had arrived, while in that time only 25,000 had been transported to other camps. That changed in the spring of 1944. During Selektion, many Jews deemed fit for work were assigned to other concentration and labor camps. The enormous network of camps imprisoned over 500,000 inmates by August 1944 and 700,000 people by December. German industry eagerly employed the slave workforce while the SS reaped massive amounts of cash paid to them by the corporations. Both of my parents were forced to labor in industries on behalf of the German war effort. But first, the Nazis had another use for my mother. She had been identified as a perfect candidate for a sadistic medical experiment.

24

ROSA IN BLOCK 10

As the SS counted the newest arrivals before leading them to their assigned block, my mother had one fervent wish: to be reunited with Celina and Sarah. She entered the camp as a laborer and was processed in the same manner as those who had come before her. She was tattooed with the number 76700. When she was shaved, the experience was every bit as inhumane as Celina's and Charles's had been. Forced to stand naked, even her eyebrows were shorn. The Nazis submitted the prisoners to full body shaves for multiple reasons: for reasons of hygiene, to prevent escape, to demoralize them by removing any remnants of human dignity or personal identity, and for monetary gain. From Berlin, the WVHA directed the camps to disinfect, dry, and pack the shaved hair in sacks so it could be sold to German companies as an industrial raw material for haircloth and felt. The Germans literally didn't waste a hair on anyone's head or body, dead or alive.

Once the registration process was completed, an SS guard began to separate the women into two groups. When my mother heard her number called, she quickly stepped to her assigned group before she could be shoved or hit by a guard. Once the guard stopped barking out numbers, she was surprised to be in the group of women led out of Birkenau and back to the main camp. She had one thought: Celina.

One day in late April 1943, Chana, a prisoner in Block 10, Auschwitz I, was placed on a special chair under the guise of a gynecological examination. After her legs were strapped into the stirrups, Nazi doctor Carl Clauberg injected a catheter containing a radioactive liquid into her uterus. This would allow him to see via X-ray whether she had any blockages in her fallopian tubes. If her tubes were clear, Chana would make an excellent specimen for the medical experiment he was conducting. The X-ray confirmed that her tubes were indeed clear, so Clauberg inserted another catheter and flushed Chana's insides with a caustic solution of five to ten percent formalin – essentially formaldehyde. To give some perspective on how toxic Clauberg's practice was, ingesting as little as 30 milliliters of solution containing 37 percent formaldehyde is enough to kill an adult. Within seconds, Chana was writhing in excruciating pain. After the war, a survivor of the experiment described the feeling of being injected, testifying: "I had terrible burning pain and the feeling that my abdomen was coming apart, nearly as if I would explode."

To aid Clauberg in studying his results, the formalin was administered with a contrast dye, allowing for easier X-ray viewing. The chemicals caused severe inflammation and Clauberg's desired result was achieved. Chana's fallopian tubes were now permanently fused and obstructed. The doctor was delighted, having personally selected Chana fresh from her cattle car since, as he put it, "Neither hunger nor disease had wiped the pink off [her] cheeks yet."

 The experiment's most common side effects were fever, peritonitis (inflammation of the membrane lining the abdominal wall and covering of abdominal organs), reproductive tract hemorrhages, multiple-organ failure, and death. Sometimes Dr. Clauberg killed his

76

subjects with a shot of phenol in the heart so he could carry out autopsies to reinforce his research. He suffered from no moral dilemmas in doing so because, in his opinion, the Jewesses at his disposal were subhuman and already condemned to death.

The women who survived Clauberg's experiments typically stayed in Block 10 for five to six weeks, allowing him to repeat his injections with a higher concentration of formalin if the first doses didn't cause the complete obstruction of the fallopian tubes. The unfortunate woman who was still fertile after her first treatment could count on three to six subsequent injections at intervals of every three to four weeks. If the subsequent injections didn't kill her, they left her incapable of working, therefore dispatching her to the gas chamber. According to the calculations of Dr. Alina Brewda-Bioloski, a Jewish prisoner forced to work in Block 10, Clauberg performed his experiments on approximately 1,000 women.

25

COMMANDANT WALTER QUAKERNACK

On April 7, 1944, the guards in Birkenau asked the male prisoners to present themselves if they were interested in volunteering for a new labor assignment. The SS were looking for men who had been employed as electricians, lathe operators, milling machinists, carpenters, and painters. They were hoping to obtain 500 workers. Only 200 came forward. The next day, the volunteers left in trucks for the 40-kilometer ride north to Laurahütte, a brand-new subcamp at the Laura Steel mill in the town of Siemianowitz. The Laura mill belonged to the Rheinmetall-Borsig AG corporation of Düsseldorf, Germany. Rheinmetall manufactured anti-aircraft guns for the German Navy. Since it was an arms plant, it was under military supervision.[1] Laurahütte's prisoners would be tasked with building the rest of the camp's infrastructure: the barracks, kitchen, secretarial office, and camp hospital. Once the structures were completed, work in the steel factory would begin.

The 200 volunteers were not sufficient to provide the manpower necessary to complete the camp as expeditiously as the Germans desired, so the following month, 300 mostly unskilled workers, almost all of them Belgian, were sent to Laurahütte to boost the labor force. My father, the former clothier to Brussels' elite, was one of them. He arrived to find a camp shaped like a triangle, with barbed wire-topped walls approximately three meters high. The subcamp's first buildings consisted of a brick building that contained the camp storehouses, and a large factory hall where prisoners would be quartered on three-tier wooden bunks. There were three watchtowers on the inside corners of the camp, and a guardhouse next to the gate through which the prisoners exited directly into the factory buildings.

Smaller transports of Auschwitz prisoners came to Laurahütte in the following months, predominantly Jews of different nationalities, including a transport of approximately 150 Jews from Hungary in September 1944, bringing the total number of prisoners to 1,000.

Recently promoted from his grisly role as the *Rottenführer* [team leader] in a Birkenau crematorium, SS *Oberscharführer* [senior squad leader] Walter Quakernack became the new camp's commandant. He was aided by Rottenführer Friedrich Wilhelm Rex.

Quakernack's beginnings in the Nazi Party reached back to his boyhood days as a member of Hitler Youth. He was a known sadist who killed prisoners for sport. One of his favorite activities at Birkenau had been to corral Jews into a large warehouse while inebriated. Then he'd mow them down with an MP-40 machine gun as he puffed on a cigarette. Afterwards, he'd laugh as he stood in his bloody uniform watching the Sonderkommando throw the bodies onto trucks bound for the ovens. "More of *our* people are dying at the front," Quakernack would say, in justification for his bloodthirsty hobby before opening fire.

One prisoner made it his business to record everything he experienced in the camps. Arthur Lehman was imprisoned at Laurahütte, where he labored as a clerk, from its inception until its evacuation in 1945. As an office worker, he came into contact with Quakernack more than any other prisoner. His nickname for the commandant was "The Lord of Life and Death." He described Friedrich Wilhelm Rex as "inhumanely abusive."

Arthur Lehmann reported in his journal that Quakernack was "completely devastated by spotted fever and excessive drinking. He suffered repeated attacks, which the Jewish prisoner doctor described as the beginning stage of delirium tremens. We suffered indescribably from his outbursts of exaggerated self-esteem or melancholy, of racial abuse and his hatred of Jews. He was a terrible bully and later, without relying on orders from higher office, murdered at least 50 of our comrades."

There is a very well-known account of a female prisoner who fought back in the undressing room of the gas chamber. It happened on October 23, 1943. An exceptionally beautiful women, Franciszka Mannheimer-Rosenberg was a Polish ballet dancer whose stage name was Franceska Mann. SS Sergeant Josef Schillinger, notorious for choking prisoners to death, and Quakernack were on duty when they suddenly stopped in their tracks, attracted by the strikingly attractive sight of Franceska taking off her right shoe. Numerous survivors attested that as soon as the dancer noticed the two men ogling her, she launched into what appeared to be a titillating and seductive striptease act. Leaning against a concrete pillar, she slowly undid her stocking and peeled it off her foot. From out of the corner of her eye she carefully observed what was going on around her. Quakernack and Schillinger were fascinated by the beautiful woman's performance and paid attention to nobody else. Their arms hung loosely at their sides, their whips, usually so active in the undressing room, dangled limply from their wrists. They did not take their eyes from the Franceska's final performance, and she was very aware of her audience. She removed her blouse and stood squarely in front of the lecherous men in her brassiere and high heels. Steadying herself against the pillar with her left arm, she bent down, and lifted her foot slightly in order to take off her remaining shoe. What allegedly happened next took place with lightning speed. Quick as a flash, she slammed the pointy heel of her shoe violently against Quakernack's forehead. He winced in pain and covered his face with both hands. At that moment, Franceska flung herself at him and made a quick grab for his pistol.[2] What is not disputed is that Franceska fired at least one shot, gravely wounding Schillinger in the stomach. Seconds later she fired another shot, most likely meant for Quakernack. Unfortunately, the bullet missed its target, hitting SS guard Wilhelm Emmerich in the leg. Franceska's act of bravery was a rallying cry. The other women began to attack the guards, scratching and biting them. Allegedly, one SS man had his nose torn off, while another was scalped. Franceska disappeared into the crowd. A panic broke out among the SS. Any moment she might reappear and aim her pistol at another of her executioners. One by one, the SS crept outside, leaving the wounded Schillinger on the floor. Then a few of them came back and dragged him hastily to the door. A third shot was fired. One of the SS men let go of Schillinger and limped to the door as fast as he could.

The light went out in the changing room and the door was bolted shut from the outside. A few minutes later, Auschwitz Commandant Rudolf Höss entered the chamber accompanied by SS men carrying machine guns and grenades. One by one, they removed the women and shot them outside. How torturous it must have been for the brave women awaiting their murders. In retaliation for Schillinger's death, the SS guards shot women at random the following evening. Thirteen prisoners were killed, four were severely wounded, and 42 received slight wounds.

Beyond dispute is that Franceska shot Schillinger, who died on the way to the hospital, and Wilhelm Emmerich, who walked with a severe limp for the rest of his life. The actions of the beautiful, doomed Franceska Mann have been the subject of debate for decades. There are at least 14 similar testimonials from Auschwitz survivors about the incident: whether it was Quakernack's or Schillinger's pistol that Franceska fired, which man's face was hit with the shoe, and how the women were murdered after the shootings. Some accounts say it was a combination of the gas chamber and machine gun fire. Others say the women were all gunned down.

———————————————

1. Rheinmetall remains in operation today producing anti-air defense products.
2. Other accounts say she grabbed Schillinger's pistol and hit him.

26

ROSA IN BIRKENAU

Rosa, young and fertile, was a prime candidate for Dr. Clauberg's study. She only spoke to me in the vaguest terms about the atrocities she suffered in Block 10, saying her reproductive organs had been messed with, and her "things" (ovaries) removed, leaving her sterile. She was lucky to leave Block 10 alive.

And there was this: Unlike many of her fellow guinea pigs who survived, but unable to fill the void of lost families through postwar childbirth, my mother had a son waiting for her. Most of the other women had watched their children go to the other line back on the Judenrampe; they soon learned they had been gassed.

Rose quickly suspected the worst about Fiszel, Celina, Albert, and Sarah. Every new prisoner's most pressing desire was to learn what had happened to their loved ones. They had seen the angry flames belching through the chimneys; the air was thick with greasy smoke that caught in the backs of their throats. Sometimes, the answer to an anxious question about the whereabouts of loved ones was as simple as a gesture towards the charcoaled sky. Hardened veteran prisoners were more direct, responding, "Up the chimney," when asked about family members. One survivor learned the fate of her parents within minutes of arriving at Birkenau. "I asked a *Kapo* [a prisoner whom the SS gave authority over other prisoners as overseers], 'When are we going to be reunited with our parents?' She pointed to one of the chimneys of the crematoria and said, 'Do you see that chimney? There go your parents, and when you go through the chimney, you'll be reunited.'"

My mother kept telling herself that no matter what had happened to Celina and her family, she had a son to return to, a reason to fight for her life. She shut out any thoughts that the Decraene's and I might not be safe. Thankfully, she wasn't aware of the danger to which Gerard regularly subjected himself; she had no reason to believe I could be harmed.

Once her fallopian tubes were wrecked and her ovaries were removed, my mother was of no further use to Clauberg. She was released from the hospital. She would have to work now, and that would burn the few calories she was allotted. In Block 10, she had spent the time laying in her bunk, which, although unheated, was at least in a brick building. In Birkenau, she'd be in a wooden barrack with a clay floor that became muddy when it rained and generated clouds of dust when the weather was dry.

When she entered her new block in Birkenau, she was assaulted by the terrible stink of the place. The primitive wooden bunks were damp with feces. Many prisoners suffered from *Durchfall*, a type of diarrhea akin to dysentery, caused by a significant drop in the level of protein and other nutrients. Adding to the sufferers' discomfort was the humiliation of soiling themselves. The women were only allowed a few minutes in the toilets before going to work and after returning in the evening. At night, the toilets were forbidden. Instead, women had to relieve themselves in buckets. Feces stuck to their buttocks and legs and dried like cracked clay. Although there were bathhouses in Birkenau, prisoners were rarely given access to them. The dreadful sanitation conditions caused skin afflictions such as scabies, boils, rashes, and abscesses. Prisoners who worked outdoors in winter were prone to frostbite in addition to their other afflictions. When they were granted use of the bathhouse, they had to undress in the barracks and walk to it naked, regardless of weather conditions. In winter, the exposure led many people, already in ill health, to more rapid deterioration and death.

The basic diet for female prisoners was unsweetened ersatz coffee, or "leaf" tea for breakfast, a bowl of soup cooked from a vile extract made of weeds or fishmeal at midday, and a slice of bread with a scoop of jam or a tiny speck of margarine in the evening. Rarely, a slice of sausage or salted curd cheese was added to the evening meal.

In an experiment with rats that were fed a diet modelled on concentration camp food, the rodents developed a typical hunger disease syndrome within three months, even if the quantity of food was unrestricted. In other words, even if the women had been given unlimited amounts of the Birkenau diet, they would still have been malnourished due to the diet's inadequate animal protein, fat, vitamins, and minerals.

In October 1947, expert witness Professor Jan Olbrycht testified for the Investigation of German Crimes in Poland: "Meals were prepared in the prison kitchen using literally all the scraps gathered while sorting products brought to Auschwitz by the people who arrived there in mass transports for extermination in the gas chambers. One cannot therefore be surprised that a soup made from such scraps would often contain buttons, razor blades, shoelaces, condoms and other similar articles."

One prisoner was so driven by his hunger that he agreed to have one of his gold teeth torn out in exchange for a slice of bread. Two unnamed prisoners attempted to break into a pigsty in order to steal pig slops. Inmates were so desperate for food that the commandant's office issued a warning for prisoners not to eat trash from the garbage dump, as rat poison had been put there.

The infamous Selektions didn't just take place at the entrance ramp. The SS conducted them routinely among the laborers, too. People who weren't economically useful to the Reich through their work contributions were exterminated. The Birkenau diet was not meant to sustain life. After all, a never-ending replenishment of labor was delivered to the Judenrampe every day. However, there was a difference between starving prisoners who had a will to live and those who had given up. The latter were referred to as *Muselmänner*, camp jargon for the walking dead. Muselmänner were totally emaciated and resigned to death – the walking dead. Their identities had been obliterated by the many dehumanizing processes of Birkenau: separation from loved ones, stripping, theft of hair, tattooing, and the physical effects of starvation, cold, disease, and physical violence.

"Everyone was in constant danger of becoming a *Muselmann*," said Władysław Kuraszkiewica, a Polish linguist who survived the camps Sachsenhausen and Orienburg. Although Kuraszkiewica was not in Auschwitz, the same held true across all the camps when it came to the Muselmänner. "All it took was to catch a slight cold or chafing on your foot from wearing the clog, get your first boil, or merely be absent-minded one day and thus attract the notice of an SS man at work or in the block. Then the first blows fall. Someone who is weakened slows the work pace, and so he is punished again. He turns into a zombie, loses his strength of will, and no longer has any control over himself – the typical image of the Muselmann."

Muselmänner did not elicit much sympathy from other prisoners. One survivor perfectly expressed the mindset these walking skeletons evoked: "Of course, we were all bags of bones, but the Muselmänner were a terror to behold. It was not just his yellow pallor which marked him out. The Muselmann was hunched, meek, resigned, and moved only with effort. There were often tears in his eyes. I averted my gaze from such prisoners because even a glance from one of them

86

might infect me. All I could feel for them was a contemptuous pity. Sympathy was a sentiment from another, lost world."

The Nazis were sticklers for efficiency. In Malines, for example, a transport was not sent to Auschwitz until the desired number of Jews was collected. The same economy was practiced to fill the gas chambers, a survivor testified after the war. "First, they went to the *revier* [infirmary] and collected all the sick. If their number fell short of the desired quantity, they went into a random block and made all the prisoners come out; they quickly separated the strongest prisoners from the weaker ones and joined the latter to the sick. Then the whole group, completely naked, was brutally loaded onto a truck."

A means of torture in every concentration camp was the *Appell*, the twice daily roll call of prisoners in front of their blocks. The term came from the German word *Appellplatz* [roll call area]. Literally, *every* body in the camp had to be accounted for, so during morning Appell, the living were responsible for dragging out the corpses of those who had died during the night. "Prisoners would be counted twice, and any discrepancies, if there was somebody missing, they started looking for that person and you could stand until they found them – 18 hours, 24 hours. If everybody tallied, if it was right, everything was all right," recalled one survivor. Another testified: "It was very cold and if you moved, they pulled you out and just shot you right there for no reason. They just went through, walked, the Germans, the SS soldiers, with sticks and constantly beating or pulling out or doing something. Either it was extremely cold or very hot. And in the evening again, it was the same thing. Twice a day."

For the sick especially, the Appell was not only physically torturous, but a matter of life and death. With prisoners neatly lined up in the rows of five abreast which the Nazis were so fond of, it was particularly easy to pluck out candidates for extermination. In attempting to save the vulnerable, inmates would stand as close to their ill friends or family members as possible, literally holding them up. Sometimes they'd link arms. One survivor recalled: "There were corpses around us – constantly. These were picked up usually during those grueling roll calls in full view for all of us of to see. These 'almost corpses' were handled like logs. Just thrown on a men-pulled wagon. But much too often they weren't really dead yet. Their arms started to flail, the eyes in their sockets moved around, like silent pleas for help. And we were not permitted to do anything, just stood there totally impotent to respond. These agonizing memories stayed with me for decades, giving me nightmares. After the war, I learned that these half dead/half alive prisoners weren't even gassed first but cremated while still breathing. Humans' inhumanity to their fellow human beings was totally unrestrained."

Evening Appell, held after prisoners were exhausted from the day's hard labor, and before their evening meal, was especially arduous. As with morning Appell, the prisoners needed to drag anybody who had died during the day so the tally would be correct. Inaccuracies stretched the Appell, was the practice was also extended as a form of punishment, sometimes lasting the entire night. To increase the agony, sometimes the guards would sometimes make the prisoners kneel while keeping their arms in the air. Even if they spent the entire night at Appell, prisoners, were still expected to put in a full day's labor the next morning.

There were two main distinctions of labor – that which was performed inside the camp perimeter, and that which was performed outside the camp. In-camp Kommandos included cleaning camp streets, clearing away corpses, removing garbage, and *Scheisskommando* [shit commando] cleaning latrines. The most privileged prisoners worked in places such as Kanada, where they could obtain food, clothing, and valuables for trading – items which could save their lives. If they were caught, however, they faced extreme punishments. The bathhouse and the laundry were also cherished assignments, being indoors and warm; the kitchen Kommando was a very plum assignment.

What one inmate may have deemed an unfavorable assignment could be another's treasure. A woman who spent two years in Birkenau demonstrated how conventional notions of status and decency were irrelevant to survival in Auschwitz. She testified: "Shifting shit was one of my happier jobs in the camp. It was a great step up in the Auschwitz world when I was drafted into the Scheisskommando. Each of the lavatory blocks had a long row of slightly raised concrete with holes. They provided a wonderful new meeting place. If you could find one of your friends during a roll call commotion, you could sit sharing a hole and talk for as long as you dared. As a matter of course there was a guard at the door to hit you going in or out. But it was worth it. In the Scheisskommando, digging out the mess from underneath and carrying it away in buckets on a yoke across my shoulders to be dumped in the pits, I had the privilege of frequent access to the toilets. This meant twenty times the conversation and organizing I'd been able to manage up till now."[1]

Unfortunately, my mother never told me what kind of labor she performed in Birkenau, and I never thought to ask her, so I am relying on the testimony of others to flesh out what was going on around her:

"Everybody was a Kommando. Each group, whatever they did, they were a Kommando. I worked in the *Leichenkommando* [corpse commando]. We said, 'What a job,' since we never saw a corpse in our lives. And we were all years old. But they told us that if we do this job, we will have plenty of food. We do not have to march, we do not have to stand at Appell which was, in itself, a murderous thing. By the time you were ready to march you were half dead from standing. We can sleep longer. So we said, 'Well, why can't we do it? If we won't do it, somebody else will. Let's try it.' And this whole group, 18 or 20 girls, said okay. And every time a corpse was lying around we just had to pick it up and put it in a certain area until they took them away. Of course it was very terrible at the beginning. And then you just did it automatically. Because things were happening all the time. You just became very... callous. You did not think. You just did what you had to do, and your main objective was not to be too tired, not to be too hungry, not to be too cold. And, unfortunately, it was a very busy job, because people were just falling like flies. The people were dying in such masses that it could not be handled."

Prisoners were often made to work beyond their strength using only their bare hands or primitive tools, with no means of transportation to and from labor assignments, which could be miles away. Often they were given senseless work to wear them down physically and mentally, such as carrying stones, bricks or mud, then returning them to their original places. They were terrorized by SS guards and Kapos who shouted at them, beat them, and applied various cruel forms of harassment to instill a constant feeling of fear, while at the same time making them perform their work faster. Most prisoners succumbed to the pressure and quickly deteriorated.

Despite the horrors surrounding and surely involving my mother, a miracle occurred. She found her sister. Celina had managed to survive for six months. She was a wizened veteran prisoner who would take my mother under her wing and do everything in her power to keep her alive. My mother and my aunt vowed to do whatever it took to remain together. In late June, they managed to do just that when together they were transferred out of Auschwitz.

---

1. The term "organizing" was camp lingo referring to the secret bartering between prisoners of items such as clothing, shoes, or food which enabled them to survive.

27

CHARLES IN LAURAHÜTTE

When Charles arrived in Laurahütte in May 1944, approximately nine SS men and 40 considerably older German marines were supporting Quakernack and Rex. The marines were downright elderly compared to the age of a typical SS guard. The Germans were losing the war and all available younger men were needed at the front. The older guards didn't treat the inmates as badly as the SS, though they still weren't averse to beating them.

The new subcamp was still under construction. The old factory had been partially destroyed by bombs in 1939; it took two weeks before it was ready for production. My father labored building the prison barracks, the infirmary, and the guard barracks. In surviving records, he was listed as a locksmith although, to my knowledge, he had no previous experience in that field. In addition to building new structures, he and the other new prisoners had to organize the storage facility – heavy labor which involved clearing enormous stones, wood, and heavy iron beams by hand. Once the camp was ready, the prisoners were trained for positions inside the factory.

The workday initially lasted for 12 hours, and a night shift was added later. The night shift was favored by the prisoners because the old marines oversaw; the SS were asleep.

"We had to get up at 5:30 in the morning and be at the factory by 6 a.m.," recalled survivor René Raindorf. After working until 6 p.m., the prisoners had one or two hours to themselves in the barracks before going to sleep. "We had discussions. I learned of the Normandy invasion[1] through the civilians who worked at the factory. They had a radio. We didn't know if the invasion had succeeded but we knew it happened. We were careful about discussing politics. You couldn't just talk to anyone."

The anti-aircraft artillery manufactured at Laurahütte was high precision equipment that required high-quality work. If a guard reported a prisoner to the SS for any alleged offenses, severe punishment was imposed on all the prisoners. Any little transgression was regarded as sabotage. One Dutch Jew was accused of laziness and sabotage because he intentionally built artillery that would malfunction. He was punished by flogging. Another Dutch Jew was accused of shirking work and feigning illness. He, too, was flogged. Laurahütte's prisoners produced five to six guns a week, which were inspected in the factory before being shipped out.

There was a benefit to working in a factory where vital work was supporting the Reich. "We had exceptional food," recalled Raindorf. "We received what the Germans called a supplement for heavy work, which was accorded to all those working for national defense. The logic which made the war machine work [was that] they needed us to work, so they had to feed us. The considerations of Selektions were put aside for later."

The better rations didn't stop some inmates from attempting to escape. Jan Purgal, a Pole, fled on the night of August 18, 1944 with another prisoner's help. The SS conducted an investigation, after which all Polish prisoners were moved to Auschwitz III-Monowitz in early September 1944. Two Jewish prisoners also escaped from the subcamp; their fate is unknown. The Germans used their flight to justify extra suffering for the remaining Jewish prisoners by subjecting them to an Appell that lasted several hours.

One of the saddest stories from Laurahütte pertained to a Russian prisoner who was just 16 years old. He attempted to escape by climbing into a wagon bound for Berlin and hiding under its contents. Unfortunately, he was discovered at the train station. He was brought to Auschwitz, where, unbeknownst to him because he couldn't understand German, he was sentenced to death. He was brought back to Laurahütte for his execution. He arrived terribly afraid of what he thought was a beating. While awaiting his punishment, he was tied up in the camp office. A few of his Russian compatriots came to comfort him. In the meantime, a factory supervisor was putting the finishing touches on the rafter in Block Four from which the boy was to hang. After the lunch break, the prisoners were ordered to line up at Block Four. They were surrounded by SS guards holding rifles, ready to fire. The residents of the town who lived near the camp noticed the heightened activity and stood at their windows. Then the condemned boy was brought out by four guards and his judgment was read out in German. Still not understanding what was being said, he laughed nervously, completely unaware of his fate. Then, to elongate the experience and build tension, his sentence was read out in French, Polish, Hungarian, and lastly, Russian, whereupon the boy began to cry. His tears incensed Quakernack, who, according to memoirist Arthur Lehman, "made a wild speech interspersed with the most unfounded words as he let the boy stand under the rope on a stool. Three prisoners who were ordered to do the business trembled so badly that the required effect did not occur. Then Rottenführer Rex grabbed the boy appropriately and Quakernack overturned the stool with a kick. The prisoners of Laurahütte were made to view the hanging body and circle around it, while Rex watched them to make sure they took a good look. The townspeople who had come to gawk stood watching, as if at a parade."

And yet, Lehman further noted: "Reports and newspapers teach us that the population knew nothing about what was going on in the camps."

Despite the risks, some prisoners were successful in resisting the Nazis. Inmates who worked in the engineering office found a way to damage the mechanisms of the artillery after it had already been inspected, thus avoiding their detection. These brave prisoners were spurred on by the busy bombing campaigns of the United States Air Force and the Royal Air Force, as well as news shared with them by Polish laborers.

On January 17, 1945, units of the Red Army advanced on outlying areas of Kraków from the north and northwest and surprised the Germans, who did not expect an attack from this flank. Kraków was just 66 kilometers west of Auschwitz. SS Chief Heinrich Himmler ordered the full evacuation of Auschwitz and its subcamps, telling camp commanders, "The Führer holds you personally responsible for... making sure that not a single prisoner from the concentration camps falls alive into the hands of the enemy."

Beginning January 15, 1944, Auschwitz began the systematic evacuation of its prisoners into Germany. These mass treks west became known as the Death Marches, when all prisoners who could walk –approximately 60,000 – were forced to march in the frigid weather without proper shoes, clothing, or food, to one of the two collection points located at railway junctions some 65 kilometers away.

On January 17, there were 937 living prisoners in Laurahütte. Referring to that day, Arthur Lehman recorded: "Around the middle of January, a train of 700 to 800 mostly Jewish prisoners on their way somewhere stopped for a few hours at our camp gate. The group had laboriously covered 12 kilometers in one day. They were worn out. The sick who couldn't go on were brought to our infirmary. The others got soup and were forced to continue. It became clear. The evacuation of the east had begun."

At Laurahütte, however, factory work continued. The subcamp was further from the Russians than Auschwitz. Incredulously, new skilled workers were even admitted to the camp during this time.

Inevitably, the evacuation order was given but the date was left to the discretion of Quakernack, in consultation with the factory management. At noon on January 22, factory work finally ceased. The prisoners were told to prepare for evacuation. Nothing that was not bolted to the ground should be left in the camp. Basically, everything was coming east except the buildings. According to Lehman, "The clothing storage gave up all its supplies – laundry, coats, even socks came to light. Everyone put on several sets of clothes to make them easier to bring with us. All materials – the portable hospital equipment, kitchen and canteen materials – were packed. That lasted until late at night, which passed in indescribable excitement."

The next morning, Quakernack went to the office to oversee the burning of all camp records. In the meantime, the wagons at the station had been lined with straw for the journey. My father was given soup, then marched through ice and snow to the train station where there was a long line of trains waiting. "There was a separate car for Aryan prisoners, and a second-class car for the captain, the company staff, and the SS," wrote Lehman. "Quakernack was at the head. The sealed wagons we rode in held anywhere from 70 to 90 people, depending on the size of the wagon." There was a car for the sick and a car for use as a kitchen canteen. "The fact that the sick were with us, which no one expected, that a kitchen wagon was set up, that we had closed wagons, not open cabbage wagons, and so many civilians in the train, gave us hope that the journey wouldn't lead to nowhere. We left Laurahütte after nine and a half months. During this time we had become terribly weak but most of us still had courage and a will to persevere. That changed later. Laurahütte was a spa in comparison."

---

1. On June 4, 1944 the Allies landed in France.

28

ROSA AND CELINA IN BERGEN-BELSEN

Rosa and Celina were transferred from Auschwitz to Bergen-Belsen, a camp established in 1940 by the German military near the small German towns of Bergen and Belsen. Originally, it had been erected to hold Allied prisoners of war. Bergen-Belsen was turned over to the SS in 1943 and transitioned into a Nazi concentration camp. Beginning in the fall of 1944, as the Allies pushed further east towards Germany, the SS deported increasingly greater numbers of prisoners from the camps in the east to Bergen-Belsen, Dachau, and other concentration camps in Germany.

In August 1944, a women's camp was established in Bergen-Belsen to absorb the masses of prisoners coming in, primarily from Auschwitz-Birkenau. Because the camp didn't have the sufficient number of Blocks to contain the new prisoners, about 8,000 women were housed in tents. The thin canvas offered them little protection from the elements. From a surviving document I found that listed Rosa and Celina in the *Zeltlager*, meaning tent camp, I know they lived in one. My mother never mentioned them.

Hetty Verolme was a survivor who spent many years of her childhood there and wrote a memoir entitled, *The Children's House of Belsen*. She recalled: "A large tent was erected on the flat ground close to the shoe pile. Soon after, we saw long columns of women [from Auschwitz] passing. They were poorly dressed. Some had no shoes at all and had their feet covered in dirty rags. Most wore some material to try and cover their bare bodies. It was eerie to watch. Their feet made no noise and they made no sound as they shuffled past. They were housed in the large tent. A few days earlier, bales of straw had arrived for them to sleep on. Many had dysentery, so one could imagine the indescribable conditions inside their tent after a few days. Our men had been ordered to dig the latrines. The latrines were in the open but the women had degenerated to the point that they did not care. All the time we could hear them fighting and screaming among themselves. Sometimes a Kapo with a whip would enter the tent and mete out a belting to those poor creatures in order to restore some peace."

I feel indebted to Hetty Verolme, who had the courage to relive what happened to her in Bergen-Belsen by recording it. Although it was hard to read, it gave me a picture of what my mother and aunt lived through. Copies of faded camp documents in which my mother's name is listed give a very flat portrait, merely proof that she was there. But the questions I beat myself up over never having asked beg for answers.

At the Arolsen Archives, formerly known as the International Tracing Service (ITS) in Bad Arolsen, Germany, there are a staggering 13 million World War II/Holocaust documents available online. From the surviving Holocaust records for Rosa Satt and Celina, I obtained a document dated June 29, 1944 that originated from Buchenwald, a major German concentration camp with almost 100 subcamps. This was one of those rare pieces of history that was much more than a name on a list. It was a report was entitled: "Concerning Examinations from June 24, 1944 – Tent Camp."

Below, it stated: "The following prisoners were today examined by a doctor and found to be fit for work and found transportable." The prisoner numbers of 775 women were listed below in neat columns. I am not sure how "fit" my mother would have been. She had recently had her ovaries shriveled to raisins by a chemical cocktail before having them excised and shipped to Berlin for research. But her prisoner number is clearly there (as is Celina's), so there is no doubt that she and my aunt were part of the tent camp. I am only guessing that they left Auschwitz on June 23 because that date lines up with the date of her medical examination.[1] This means my mother was only in Birkenau for about two weeks. Most women in Clauberg's program stayed in Block 10 for about six weeks. I can only speculate that she was experimented on immediately after arriving, and that the desired sterilization was achieved after the first dose of formalin. She'd been a model subject.

My mother's stop in Buchenwald on the way to Bergen-Belsen made no sense to me, so I turned to Vincent Slatt, a reference librarian and archivist at the USHMM. I had already listened to oral histories and read testimonies by other survivors who had traveled the same trajectory as my mother and aunt; none of them had alluded to a short stop in Buchenwald for a medical examination. Vincent told me, "In the last months of the war the transfers between camps increased and included a lot of transfers from Auschwitz into the camps within Germany. Many of these subcamps were in the armaments industry and there was a major push for people that would work to support the war effort. It is highly possible that she was deemed able to work and used in this fashion. Further, we know that transfers weren't necessarily from Auschwitz directly to a work site, but often to camps along the way, where further selections were made and people were separated from some groups and added onto other groups for further travel. It is not uncommon for multiple people to share the same path of persecution, as the other testimony you identified, but these tend to be a few people out of the hundreds of transfers."

I found this helpful. It now made sense that my mother's path *didn't* make sense – including the fact that the document listed the women as being from the Zeltlager. The tent camp was in Bergen-Belsen, so if they were labeled as the women from the Tent Camp, they'd come to Buchenwald from Bergen-Belsen. Perhaps they'd been yo-yoed back and forth between the two camps – Auschwitz-Birkenau to Bergen-Belsen to Buchenwald, and back to Bergen-Belsen. It's another mystery I'll never solve.

What is certain is that Rosa and Celina were living in a tent as winter was approaching. Ironically, it was the severe German weather – which should have diminished their ability to survive – that saved them. A violent storm destroyed most of the tents on November 7, 1944. "A storm blew away the big tent in which the women of Auschwitz were housed," wrote Hetty Verolme. "In the wind and pouring rain those poor women stood without any protection against nature's brute force. Most of them were without clothing or shoes and were soaked wet to the bone. They looked like white ghosts in the downpour." The SS were forced to find new living quarters for the women; they were rehoused in wooden barracks akin to those in Birkenau. Also reminiscent of Birkenau was the punishment of withholding food if the SS found even a tiny speck of dirt in the block, though the women weren't beaten and they didn't have to work. The abuse they suffered was hunger. Food was a constant on everyone's mind. The women passed the long hours "cooking," sharing favorite recipes and arguing over cooking methods. "No, you need eight of that, six of that." One survivor recalled that the inactivity was its own kind of torture. "Work was hard but it was better than sitting there and doing nothing. Your only job was to delouse yourself all day long."

Many women did not spend much time in Bergen-Belsen. As Vincent Slatt stated, the Germans urgently needed labor in armaments factories, and Bergen-Belsen needed to purge the camp before tens of thousands of retreating survivors marched in from the east. In the face of the Red Army advance, Bergen-Belsen, due to its geographical position inside the German Reich, became more and more of a destination for the evacuation transports. At the beginning of December 1944, there were around 15,000 prisoners in the camp; by February 1, 1945, there were 22,000.

I don't know precisely when my mother and aunt left Bergen-Belsen, but I do know they were among 500 women transferred as slave laborers to an airplane factory in Aschersleben, Germany, possibly on January 1, 1945, according to a Bergen-Belsen website. It's not surprising that this date does not align with my research or the testimony of one of the women in the group, who said, "I think it was the middle of January of 1945 when a civilian came. He had on a brown hat and a brown winter coat. And he stood outside, and he wanted 500 women to work somewhere. And [my friends and I] looked at each other. Maybe there is something better there. Should we try to get into this transport? And we got into that transport [in the] middle of January 1945. And we left Bergen-Belsen by cattle car."

Rosa and Celina also volunteered to try their luck at a camp where labor could lead to survival. One of the women called volunteering as "the first time we had the opportunity to take our fate into our own hands, and it worked out well – as well as could be expected while imprisoned under the brutal Nazi regime."

---

1. It took one day to get from Auschwitz to Bergen-Belsen.

29

CHARLES IS EVACUATED FROM LAURAHÜTTE

When Charles and his fellow prisoners were evacuated from Laurahütte, they were not told their destination. After traveling a short distance, the train stopped at Tichau Station; the engineer had spotted a military transport on one of the tracks. Arthur Lehmann hopped out and ran along the wagons knocking on the doors of the cars, enquiring about the health of the passengers. He spotted a paper attached with adhesive to each wagon which mapped out the route and destination of the trains. They were heading for Mauthausen. Lehmann later wrote in his postwar diary: "It was a nasty discovery. Mauthausen was the epitome of horror and cruelty and torture for Dutch Jews." Lehmann was from Amsterdam.

The military trains spotted by the engineer had been sighted by British aircraft and an attack was expected. The SS aimed their anti-aircraft weapons at the sky in preparation. The Laurahütte train sped out of the station only to halt 20 minutes later due to a route closure in a forest near the station in Rzedówka. The SS used the time to fetch water from the farms close to the edge of the forest to resupply the kitchen wagons; they left with some inmates and kitchen workers. Soon, they returned and waved for the rest of the prisoners to join them. They had stumbled upon a convoy of deserted, open-doored coal wagons. Rubble of all kinds surrounded the area: torn prisoner uniforms, steel helmets, bowls, SS helmets covered in blood, broken rifles, blank index cards used in the camp offices, record books with pages torn out, and corpses in striped prison clothing. The SS ordered the group to inspect the wagons. In the hospital car, they found two, barely alive, faintly whimpering Jews who were hidden under the detritus of broken beds. They were so close to death they could hardly speak. Not only were they ill, starving, and extremely parched, they were nearly and literally frozen. Quakernack remarked, "It must be a prisoner transport that has been attacked by partisans."[1] Quakernack wouldn't allow them to pursue the trail of clothing and equipment leading into the forest. Rather, he directed them to collect the books and cards, not wanting damning records to fall into Allied hands. He also instructed them to remove and collect the uniforms from the corpses and any bowls found lying on the ground. The two barely breathing survivors were placed in a wheelbarrow and brought to the car reserved for corpses, directly behind the ambulance car.

The departure whistle blew, signaling it was time to leave. The door to the corpse car was frozen shut, but the ambulance car was open, so the two frozen men were placed there. In time, they thawed enough to tell the prisoners what had transpired. Their transport of about 1,000 Jews had been exterminated in the wagons and the forest by the accompanying SS, who then fled. The two men were the only survivors. Later, Holocaust researchers deduced that the dead were probably prisoners from the Günthergrube subcamp of Auschwitz.

Every morning of the journey, the trains came to a stop. Arthur Lehmann had the job of walking down the row of cars to see if anyone had died. When the wagon doors were open, he wrote later, "Each time the picture was the same of the poor, starved, thirsty, depraved people who huddled against the wagon door to catch a few breaths of fresh air." Four men from each wagon were allowed to drag the dead away, and four were dispatched to the kitchen cart to get bread for their fellow inmates. They were given no water to drink. Instead, the SS pushed snow through the slats of the wagon walls.

While the Jews were starving and shivering in the wagons, Quakernack was having a delightful journey. On the second day, he visited the civilian car, where he pulled a woman out of her seat and brought her back to his quarters; he used her to satiate his sexual desires for the remainder of the trip. "His Imperial German Killer slept and lived with her as if nothing was happening," wrote Lehmann sarcastically. The couple was "looked after like a noble servant by the German prisoner of honor, Erhard Jacobi, a terrible bully and notorious car thief in civilian life. In the morning he ran down to Quakernack's train with a breakfast tray. And that was repeated at noon and in the evening."

When the train finally reached Mauthausen, Austria at 4 a.m. on January 29, there were 135 corpses among the barely living prisoners, a very high number. But considering how low the temperatures were in the open wagons and how malnourished the prisoners were, it's a wonder that figure wasn't higher.

From the small rail station, the prisoners could see a snow-covered landscape framed by tall mountains. The beauty of the scene seemed to mock their misery. How could the world contain such loveliness in conjunction with so much evil and misery?

The somnolent SS men waiting to receive the prisoners came to life, roughly kicking them out of the wagons. But before departing for the camp, an Appell was held. Once that ordeal was over, the dead were thrown in the same trucks as the seriously ill. Some of the men were so weak, yet still maintained the strong will to live. They staggered and crawled to the trucks reserved for the able-bodied, mustering up the last of their strength to avoid joining the corpses. Nonetheless, they received violent kicks for their efforts and were dumped in with the dead.

The town of Mauthausen seemed deserted. The men plodded through a forest, past huge stone quarries, and uphill for over an hour. Those who couldn't keep up simply crumpled silently into the snow and were left behind. Finally, the thick walls of the camp appeared and the prisoners marched through yet another gate.

New camp, same routine. The men were stripped, showered, and deloused. According to survivor Charles Strassberg's video testimony, a doctor examined them and made some sort of notation on the backs of their necks that indicated whether they were capable of working. Dripping wet and naked, they were shoved outside in the freezing temperatures and endured a long march to an unfinished barrack where they were registered and finally given tattered, dirty, threadbare, striped uniforms that were grossly inferior to the clothes they had been wearing when they had marched into the camp, the extra layers they'd procured from Laurahütte's stores. After a meal of watery soup they fell onto the floor to sleep – utterly spent.

The next day they were awakened by Mauthausen's curious veteran inmates, who had come to inspect the new arrivals and see if they had any goods to organize. Did anyone have some bread to trade for maybe a warm shirt? Or some gold that could be traded for food? What about paper? Paper, which was used to insulate clothing, might be good for trading if someone wanted it enough to trade his bread for it.

The established prisoners quickly deduced that the Laurahütte group was of little use to them, so they turned instead to the business of initiating the new men with scary Mauthausen horror stories, which were so bad that they made the men shake – tales of death by gassing or petroleum injections, for example. But the newcomers had a short time to reflect on the horrors at Mauthausen. By late the next evening, they were ordered to line up on the camp road and march downhill in the deep snow; they found it as difficult as the march uphill had been. Still, they were relieved to be leaving and it gave them some measure of strength. The march was only five kilometers.

In two hours, they passed through yet another gate to a brightly lit Appell area. They were in a Mauthausen subcamp: Gusen II. Its reputation was worse than Mauthausen's.

---

1. In fact, Nazis had committed the massacre, which he probably suspected but would never admit to the prisoners.

30

ROSA AND CELINA IN ASCHERSLEBEN

One day after my mother and aunt climbed aboard the cattle car in Bergen-Belsen they arrived in Aschersleben, a small town in the industrial heartland of Germany where a branch factory of the Junkers Flugzeug-und-Motorenwerken [Junkers Aircraft and Engine Company] was located. A men's camp had already been established there the previous summer. Both the men's and the women's camps were subcamps of Buchenwald. Transferred with Rosa and Celina were 250 Poles, 232 Hungarians, 11 other Belgians, a German, a Soviet, a Yugoslav, and two Slovaks. The SS guards of the men's camp were also charged with guarding the external perimeters of the women's camp. At the women's camp, 12 female SS guards, described by survivors after the war as "downright brutal," guarded the interior of the camp.

The women were given thin black coats painted with their new prisoner numbers and marched to their new barracks. When they entered, they were stunned by what they saw. Compared to Birkenau, the barrack seemed regal. It was heated with huge hot water pipes running through the rooms. The bunks held single-bed straw mattresses which did not need to be shared, unless one counted the bedbugs. The women even had hot shower facilities, which they were allowed to use every day. "It was beyond our wildest dreams," recalled a survivor. The quality and quantity of the food was also better, though it was still insufficient. My mother marveled at the bits and pieces of meat and potato swimming in her thin soup, and the larger ration of bread to dip into it.

For all its upgrades, Aschersleben was still a concentration camp, and every day began with Appell, but it was dealt with quickly. Then the women worked 12-hour-day or evening shifts in the factory, assembling fuselages and cutting and assembling aircraft parts, "Hard work, but survival was possible," recalled one of the women. "We worked alongside hundreds of other workers, some of them Polish and Ukrainian forced laborers who were paid and lived in the town of Aschersleben. I think the majority of them were non-German and many of them were POWs. Some were Flemish volunteers from Belgium, sympathizers with Nazism. My foreman, a French POW, warned me about them. He was kind. Every time he wanted to indicate to me that something hopeful is happening, very, very quietly he'd sing the *Marseillaise*, the French national anthem. We had to be very careful." The female SS guards were always watching from the gallery, but they didn't always catch everything. According to a survivor who was tasked with testing pipes, "We sabotaged that work with the knowledge of the German foreman, Otto Riesener." According to my mother, covert resistance in the form of sabotage was very common in Aschersleben.

Each shift was allotted two breaks and the prisoners worked right alongside the civilians. According to a survivor, "There were about 120 Ukrainian women who also worked in that factory, who were *Freiwillige*, volunteer workers who came to help the Nazi war effort. There were also Belgian war prisoners, but there were also some Belgian volunteers, over on the Nazi side." There were paid employees from other countries, as well. "They were free. And they helped us a lot. They would give us a little piece of bread, whatever they could," testified another survivor soon after the war. If the paid employee was caught giving a prisoner food, the prisoner was punished, but the employee was not. Favorite punishments of the SS consisted of shaving the prisoners' heads, beating them, keeping them in seclusion, and withholding meals. Special tortures were meted out where the entire camp was punished: sleep-depriving, Appells lasting many hours, and debilitating calisthenics, which further exhausted the already physically weak women.

Brutal as punishments were, Aschersleben was a vast improvement over a death camp. For the first time for many of these women there were instances of humanity, as evidenced by a story survivor Judy Cohen shared in her memoir, *A Cry in Unison.*

"Listen to the irony of the Nazi hierarchy," she said. "The Ukrainian women had their own washroom. [On the door] it said *Ostarbeiterin* [female worker from the east]. The German women who worked in the office had their own toilet. They wouldn't share a washroom with the Ukrainian women who came to help them in the war effort. Lo and behold, the 500 Jewish women arrived and the Ukrainian women had to share the toilet with the Jews. Well, the Ukraines [sic] were so angry they had to share the washroom with Jews. They weren't very nice to us in the beginning. I still believe today that the toilet is a great equalizer, because something happened there that didn't happen anywhere else. Some of the Jewish women who worked with aluminum learned how to make pots and pans with lids from the scraps that fell away. They learned soldering. They learned welding. And instead of making airplanes, whenever they could, in secret, they made pots and pans. And they were trading in the toilet with the Ukrainian women, who were getting paid. So there was some business going on in that toilet. At one point, I was given a job to work with ebonite pieces. And I learned to make combs. All I needed was a saw and I could make combs. We did everything we could to trade in the toilet. And the Ukrainian women brought potatoes and carrots. And we hit it off and became friends."

Because the prisoners were working with so many civilians, war news reached them quickly. My mother was aware that the Allies had landed and the Americans were close. Sometimes, she was even able to read a smuggled newspaper. Further cheering her were the Allied planes she could see attacking during her walks to and from the factory. According to postwar SS testimony, the last day the women worked was March 25, 1945. Then the factory closed following heavy bombing raids on the town. The women had been spending more time in the air raid bunkers than in the factory, and when the raids gained in intensity, the factory work ceased.

On March 31, "One glorious Saturday morning," recalled Judy Cohen, "the planes came so fast that we didn't have time to go to the bunkers, and the bombing started. The SS guards were running around cursing because we stood in the doorways of our barracks and were so happy. We actually saw the bombs falling and nothing happened to us. From the air pressure a few windows were broken but that's it. We were laughing and giggling, saying, 'Oh, this is the end, this is the end!' while the SS were running around, yelling '*Verfluchte Juden* [cursed Jews].' They were scared. They couldn't run to the bunker because they weren't allowed to leave us alone. After that raid was over everything was leveled. In the distance we heard stored ammunition blowing up. It was magnificent. The factory was totally in ruins."

31

CHARLES IN GUSEN II

Sometimes the Germans called Gusen II by its other names: *Bergkristall* [rock crystal] and Project B-8. The prisoners had another name for it: The Hell of Hells.

The B-8 project began. in March 1944, intended as the mass production site of Messerschmidt 262 jet fighters. Had the site been completed, it would have been one of the largest German underground manufacturing facilities, 50,000 square meters of manufacturing space, all out of the sight of Allied bombers. In spite of the facility's incompletion, the mostly Polish and Hungarian prisoners in Gusen II were already producing fuselages there by early 1945. More prisoners were interned in this lesser known camp than in the main Mauthausen camp. Survivor Yechezkel Harfenes gave an account of the catastrophic conditions during the construction of the Bergkristall. "After two months we were mere wrung rags. Hunched over creatures dragging legs swollen by malnutrition. We were literally skin and bones. Our jaws and eyes protruded from yellow skulls. Once someone reached this point, it was only a matter of time before he was selected for extermination. Thousands died this way, not to mention the dozens of deaths daily from accidents, beatings, and starvation. Yet we never lacked for workers. Every month a new transport would bring thousands of new Jewish prisoners to replenish the ranks of those who had died in the past month. Work continued apace, and often in the sixteen hours that passed from the time we finished until we returned for the next shift, the place had changed so much as to be unrecognizable."

At least 71,000 people were deported to Gusen II, of whom almost 40,000 died. It was completely nonsensical that the SS would treat the men who produced their much-needed war materiel so viciously. While there was a never-ending, and thus, disposable, supply of incoming manpower, the time needed to train the new prisoners, who themselves were weakened within days, was certainly counterproductive to the German war aim.

Charles arrived just in time to witness the camp commandant raging about the discrepancy between the number of prisoners in the quarry commando who had marched out that morning and the number who had returned. The punishment, he shouted, would be an amount of men executed to equal the discrepancy. Charles saw immediately that Gusen II was going to be as terrifying or worse than Mauthausen was rumored to be.

After the initiation with the commandant, the men were split into two quarantine barracks and allowed to sleep for a few hours. After resting, they were given hot liquid and bread. The Block Elder introduced himself by beating some of the men to death. After that performance, the men were told to disrobe. They were given new identification numbers – strips of fabric that were sewn onto their new uniforms, and bracelets with the corresponding number plate attached to a piece of wire. Next came a lice check. Despite having been deloused the previous day at Mauthausen, some of the men were still afflicted, so they all had to march for 20 minutes to the washhouse for another treatment. Their new uniforms went into the steam room for disinfection and the men were sprayed with a delousing agent. Next, they were ordered to parade with their arms in the air in front of an SS man for inspection. It appeared as if he was checking to make sure they were lice-free, but actually, he was making notes for a forthcoming Selektion. Then the men showered and were shaved. After exiting the hot room, they were dispatched outside, wet and naked, for the 20-minute walk back to the barracks in sub-zero temperatures. The exposure killed a number of them.

The Block Elder was creative in his cruelty. Arthur Lehmann recorded in his diary, "Meanwhile, dinner was served. We lined up in the barrack and were counted. Then the Block Elder counted the number of pieces of bread. Two servings were missing. Another count brought the same result. 'No,' decided the Block Elder. 'Nothing is missing, but there are two too many people.' And with that he grabbed a stool and hit two people with it until they were dead. Now the distribution of dinner could begin. 'It now tabulates exactly!' said the satisfied Block Elder. That was Gusen."

"As a resident of many camps, Gusen was the worst," recalled Yechezkel Harfenes. "That is not to say that conditions at the other camps were not dreadful. Compared to Gusen, however, one might almost say that those camps were paradises. The proof of this might be that Gusen was one of the least known camps. This was not because it was smaller than the others – it might even have been the largest. It is unknown simply because very few of the tens of thousands of prisoners sent there remained alive to tell the story of its horrors." In fact, so many inmates from the evacuated camps came to Gusen II via its direct railway connections that the SS began to exterminate them simply by keeping them sealed in their cars. Within days, they were frozen to death.

On February 1, 1945, after spending an event-filled day and night in Gusen II, Charles and about 500 other men were selected for another transfer. They had evidently passed the Selektion the previous day and were needed for the production of anti-aircraft guns for the firm Hannover Maschinebau Actien-Gesellschaft, aka Maschinebau A.G., known more familiarly as Hanomag. The factory was in the industrial area of Hannover, Germany. There were five other Hannover subcamps in the area, each under the auspices of the Neuengamme concentration camp. The Laurahütte men were dispatched to the subcamp Hannover-Mühlenberg-Linden, which had been in operation since 1942. (The camp had many monikers: Hannover-Linden, Hannover-Mühlenberg, Hanomag/Linden, and Hanau.) The men would be doing essentially the same work they had done in Laurahütte and therefore would require no retraining. They received two loaves of bread, a little margarine, and some sausage for the journey, as well as new blue and white striped coats.

As they marched out of the gates, the group was dismayed to see Quakernack and his staff waiting to accompany them. Any relief they had felt in leaving Gusen II instantly evaporated.

32

EVACUATION FROM ASCHERSLEBEN

After Allied bombs wiped out the airplane factory, the women feared the SS would kill them; they were no longer supporting the Reich. If they couldn't be of any use, would the SS allow them to live?

After a few days of idleness, their fears were realized when an Oberscharführer from Buchenwald arrived with some officers. "I have orders to take you all back to Buchenwald to be executed," he told the women. "They are not going to just *let* you survive." He waited a beat for the terrifying news to sink in before he added dramatically, "But I won't do it." In a matter of seconds, the women had been sentenced to death and given a stay of execution. "But you can't stay here," he continued. "Gather your belongings and prepare to march out of the camp." He assigned two armed Wehrmacht guards to accompany them. Where were they to go, the women asked.

"Just go," said the Oberscharführer without further directions. "Just march and go. Just leave."

Why were the women's lives spared? There are many possible reasons. Knowing the war was lost, perhaps the Oberscharführer wanted a little less murder on his record or even his conscience. Maybe he was just tired, and the thought of marching 500 emaciated women to Buchenwald was distasteful to him. With the Reich unraveling at every turn, he probably knew he could get away with disobeying orders. (Indeed, during the postwar Nazi trials, an oft-heard excuse by even Adolf Eichmann, the architect of the Final Solution, was: "I was just obeying orders.")

The women scrambled to collect what little personal items they had. My mother didn't even have shoes; her feet were wrapped in newspapers. A paltry amount of food was divided among them, but not nearly enough to sustain them for a prolonged march. It wasn't a trip to Buchenwald for extermination, but it was meant to kill them through starvation and exhaustion. One aspect of the march set it far apart from the Death Marches of January, of which they'd been spared. They were marching in mild April weather.

My mother and my aunt marched out of Aschersleben on April 11, 1945. One woman recalled: "Everyone had bundles of stuff – whatever they could find – like you see in the pictures, the wandering Jews." Shortly into the march, an escaped war prisoner ran by. He quietly told the women that the Americans were only three kilometers away. The news brought joy, but sadly, the Wehrmacht guards made them march in the opposite direction. The women were bitterly disappointed to come so close to liberation only to have it snatched away. Many of them wept.

"It was a never-ending road," recalled Judy Cohen, "paved with utter, unadulterated misery. We went along highways and byways. We went through little towns... We went through small forests – wherever the two guards led us. Food, whatever we took with us from camp was quickly gone. We received absolutely nothing, no food or water. We didn't even have the opportunity to relieve ourselves properly. The hunger was unbearable, relentless. We marched endlessly and aimlessly – another special torture of the Nazis. Likewise did the *Toten Kommandos* [killing squads] of the SS in their black uniforms. They were hunting and shooting prisoners like us at random at night. We lived in constant fear for our miserable lives. I have no idea how long the march lasted. Maybe eight days or less. We had no calendar and after a while we stopped counting the days. We marched and starved, starved and marched. We lived and acted like animals. Raiding garbage cans, begging, eating rotten, dirty vegetables dug from the fields."

Another marcher, Nechama Epstein-Kozlowski, testified: "While walking we picked up from the field raw potatoes when the Germans weren't looking [because] we'd be beaten. Many ate the potatoes, and many ate the peeling of the potatoes. We would pull out [of the ground] a beetroot. And on that we subsisted."

My mother and my aunt leaned on each other to stay alive. When one said she couldn't go on, the other summoned her own strength to "lift" her up, and vice versa. The women marched all day, and on a night when they happened to be in a small town, their guards would ask the town's mayor to let them sleep in an empty barn. "There were many empty barns because the German farmers didn't know which army would reach their town first – the Americans or the Russians," said Judy Cohen. "They feared the Russians terribly, and many families just left. Most of the time, the mayors refused and we had to lie down under the sky and stars on the outskirts of town. [One] particular night we happened to sleep in an abandoned, dirty stable. It had a roof and four walls and some damp straw on the earthen floor. After having slept outdoors for days this seemed like heaven, albeit a rotten one."

The women even spent a night in an empty jail. Soon, they were infested with lice everywhere they had hair, especially their armpits, which was particularly uncomfortable. If they weren't marching, they spent the time resting and picking lice off themselves and each other. Sometimes they marched out in the open through little towns that didn't appear touched by the war in any way. The women found it surreal to walk past tidy houses, their front gardens dotted colorfully with flowers freshly sprung from the soil. When civilians witnessed the rags hanging from the group's emaciated bodies, they seemed to look right through them, as if they weren't there. Nazi Germany was peppered with groups of Jewish marchers as more and more groups filtered in from the east. "Every day we saw marchers like ourselves, in striped clothing, dragging themselves on the other side of the road, going in the opposite direction," said Judy Cohen. "There was this unbelievable, no-rhyme-or-reason marching during the last few weeks before the end of the war."

One day, the women were marched through a little forest when they encountered the gunned-down bodies of men and women in striped uniforms. Rosa looked at every male corpse and thanked God that Charles wasn't among them. At least the guards weren't shooting *them*, perhaps taking a page from the Oberscharführer's book, but the women were slowly dying from starvation. Some couldn't go on. They drifted behind and fell to the ground. Every day the group shrank. Some women died of hunger, some of disease, and some of total exhaustion. Some women simply lost the will to live and just fell by the wayside. I hope some managed to escape. If my mother hadn't had Celina; if Celina hadn't had my mother, I doubt either would have survived.

In one town, at the end of one day's march, the mayor permitted the group to use a large, abandoned barn to sleep in. There was a thin layer of straw on the earthen floor. By now, the number of women had dwindled considerably. They were hungry and exhausted and had nothing to eat or drink; they dropped to the ground and fell asleep. The next morning, they were awaked by a loud knock. None of the women moved. The knocking continued, more insistently. Finally, one of the women opened the heavy door, blinking at the streaming sunlight. A tall man stood at the opening. All the women could see was his dark silhouette. In a pleasant, strong voice he addressed them in German: "*Fräulein!*" The group was shocked. No one had addressed them in a civil manner in years. They were used to being called *Verfluchte Juden, Dreckige Juden* [cursed Jews, dirty Jews]. Had he really said Fraulein? Many of the women began to cry, absorbing the implication of a polite address from a German. The man continued. *"Fräulein, Sie sind frei."* [Ladies, you are free.] It was Saturday, May 5, 1945. As their eyes became accustomed to the light, the former prisoners recognized the man as the mayor who had given them permission to sleep in the barn the previous night. Their guards were nowhere in sight.

"Fräulein, kommen sie nach draußen." [Ladies, come outside.] The women did as they were told, shielding their eyes from the sun. All around them, white flags hung from windows, replacing the red and black Nazi party flags.

Words were as far as the mayor was willing to go, however. He didn't offer them any food, not even a drink of water. Anxious to be rid of them, he told them that they were free to leave. "There are two roads you can follow from here. If you take this road," he said, indicating one direction, "ten kilometers from here are the Russians. If you take that road, six kilometers from here are the Americans."

Rosa and Celina, filthy, lice-ridden, weary, starving, and elated, clung to each other and wept.

My mother always maintained that she was liberated by the Russians, although why she and Celina would have chosen to walk ten kilometers rather than six in their weakened state doesn't make sense. Perhaps they thought they would be able to communicate more easily in Russian than in English. A few days later, on May 8, the Germans capitulated. The Third Reich kaput. A month later, the Allies divided Germany up into zones, and the area became part of the Soviet Zone. Perhaps that's what my mother meant when she told me she'd been liberated by the Russians.

According to Judy Cohen, "A serious problem developed. We learned that the Soviet soldiers were coming straight from the front... and they were taking the liberty of raping women, mainly German women, but any woman would do. Some of the soldiers came to our barracks, very drunk, and wanted to have sex with us, even forcefully. We were jumping out through the windows to escape from them. At first we were scared. Then we were outraged. The morning after this incident, a few girls went to the Soviet military command to complain. The soldiers received very strict instructions not to touch us, and it never happened again." My mother told me that she and Celina were never raped. There was a Jewish officer, she said, who made sure they were treated properly by the Russian troops. She was probably nowhere near Judy Cohen by that time.

33

CHARLES IN HANNOVER

Charles marched quietly through the deep, crunching snow to the Mauthausen train station. There stood the familiar wagons, but the kitchen and hospital cars were conspicuously absent. It was a foreshadowing of things to come. In Aschersleben, Rosa and Celina had found an improvement in the quality of their imprisonment; my father would be given no such reprieve from his miserable circumstances. He climbed wearily aboard the cattle car and settled on the hard boards for another long journey. Within three hours, the convoy exited Austria through the border town of Passau, Germany. The train continued through Hof, around Leipzig, over Magdeburg, past Hildesheim, and into Hannover. What should have been an 11-hour trip took two days. The rails had been heavily bombed, causing the course to be diverted repeatedly. For the duration of the trip, the prisoners were given water just once. "We stopped at the train station in Hannover-Linden on the afternoon of February 5," Arthur Lehmann incorrectly recorded in his diary, though the journey must have felt like it had lasted an extra day. "Miraculously, everyone had survived," he continued. "But we were semi-insane, apathetic, starved, and generally in an indescribably run-down condition."

Once freed from the cars, the men gulped in lungsful of clean air. Seeing the area's bombed-out devastation revived Charles slightly. "The prospect of getting back to a somewhat orderly labor camp gave [us] new courage," recalled Arthur Lehman. The prisoners, 95 percent of them Jewish, were marched through the town past townspeople who were openly hostile to them. What they saw when they came through the gates at Hannover quickly sank any hopes for an orderly camp. The Italian forced laborers who had been there before them left the camp in an "indescribably dirty condition," wrote Arthur Lehmann. "Most of the windows and doors were missing, toilets were broken, water and light pipes were cracked and separated, and the floor of the barracks was so muddy that you sank in it up to your ankles."

There were no beds or blankets. The inmates spent the first night on the muddy floor. The next day, straw sacks and blankets were delivered. The men had to carry them from the railroad cars with the help of a truck. Kommandos were formed, charged with marching into the city to scavenge useful materials from the bombed-out detritus of the town: windows, doors, and rubble. The rubble was mixed with the mud on the floors as a makeshift recipe for cement. Wooden sleeping bunks, the ubiquitous three-tiered skeletons, were also constructed from materials salvaged from the town. "Because everything was in such a state of disrepair, the inmates were set to work making the camp inhabitable. Fencing had to be mended and electrified, searchlights erected, and toilets and washbasins repaired," Arthur Lehmann wrote. They were in such a physically weakened and starving state that the heavy work, basically rebuilding the camp upon arrival, killed some of them. "There was only thin soup and bread to eat that you could see the sun through," recalled one survivor.

According to camp records, seven inmates died in the first week. When the camp was finished being readied, it consisted of eight barracks that were surrounded by a thick, electric, barbed wire fence. One barrack served as a combination camp office/living room for the guards, one as a kitchen/living room for the Kapos, one as a toilet and washroom, and one as a 40-patient infirmary, albeit one with only enough beds for the sick to sleep two to a bed, and no medicine. The other four barracks housed the prisoners. Each building had two rooms on either side, with about 35 triple-tiered bunks, an oven, and a table with benches for perhaps ten people. The Block Elder was entitled to a cupboard. There were two blankets for each bed – one as a sheet and one as a cover – but the blankets were never laundered and quickly became infested with vermin, as was the prisoners' clothing. Most of the men didn't have shoes, so they made do by wrapping rags around their feet.

On February 12, the men began work in the factory where they continued the production of anti-aircraft weapons. In Laurahütte, they provided slave labor to Rheinmetall-Borsig. It is not completely clear whether Hanomag or Rheinmetall-Borsig requested the inmates. Of the two firms, Rheinmetall most likely continued to "employ" the Laurahütte inmates; the company may have rented two work halls in the Hanomag factory to continue its anti-aircraft weapons production. Even though the men labored in the Hanomag factory, they were most likely working for the same company they had worked for at Laurahütte. In the archives of both companies, there is no documentation that clarifies which company benefited from the extortion.

The prisoners were guarded by civilian foremen in the factory, but the SS were always around, patrolling the halls and carrying out drastic punishments. For example, prisoners were not allowed to speak, and whoever did ran the risk of being clubbed to death. Many guards wanted to make a name for themselves in order to evade being sent to the front. By now, no one cared to give up his life for Hitler (who was less than two months away from committing suicide). As a result, the inmates were mercilessly screamed at, beaten, and kicked. The violence began as soon as the men reached Hannover. A prisoner named Wolf Sonnenschein was not up on his feet fast enough one morning, so he fell under the blows and kicks of the SS. When his glasses fell on the ground, the guards smashed them with the heels of their boots. Being extremely short-sighted, Wolf was completely helpless without them. He was pushed into the washroom and sprayed with cold water until he lay on the floor. The next morning his body was still there.

According to Arthur Lehman, the work in the Hannover factory was no harder than at Laurahütte, "But people stood in the half-destroyed halls all day long in freezing temperatures, draft, and often in rain," due to the factory's walls having been virtually destroyed by bombs. During lunch, Charles chewed his bread ration slowly to make it last longer. It was smaller than the piece he had gotten for breakfast. The men were forbidden to sit down while eating. They hadn't been off their feet since they'd woken. To get to the factory, they'd had to walk almost three kilometers. For most of the men, the trek depleted what fragile reserves they had before their 12-hour shifts even began. After the workday ended, they were forced to run through the camp gates as the camp elder hit them arbitrarily with a hammer, killing some of them.

"Every day, people collapsed. The [collapsed] were driven [back] to camp on carts and brought to life by the SS with rubber truncheons or iron sticks filled with sand. If that didn't [revive them], the camp leader or one of his cronies took pity," elaborated Arthur Lehmann sarcastically. "Head-down immersion in rain barrels was a popular means that was almost always invigorating. Usually that led to a death report."

Conditions went from poor to barely survivable. "The deterioration of the camp was very bad. From Neuengamme, there was never any inspection or any kind of control. The commandant of [subcamp] Hannover-Stöcken only came once during our second month. The delivery of food – cabbage, potatoes, and bread, sometimes cheese, was very irregular, which led to great tension. Underwear and clothing never came. For the first two weeks, there was no medical care. Finally the medic from the district SS health service came with a doctor who had bandages and medicine," wrote Arthur Lehmann.

By the second and third weeks, 38 more prisoners had died. The next month, the mortality rate decreased slightly; in the weeks from February 27 to March 13, 19 deaths were recorded; between March 12 to March 14, 17 more people died. The men suffered from pneumonia, starvation, edema, diarrhea, and exhaustion. As the end of the war intensified, there were air raids three times a day. All prisoners were driven into underground tunnels with lashes from whips and sticks. They spent hours in the damp, cold air. Some stood in groundwater.

When the prisoners first reached Hannover, corpses were packed in paper sacks and trucked to the city for cremation. By March 8, the undertaker refused to collect any more "like cattle" from the camp. To control the mass of corpses, the SS made the prisoners stack the bodies cordwood-style in the camp's morgue until they could be buried in pits within Hannover-Linden's borders.

Meanwhile, the Allies stepped up their air attacks in the heavily industrial region, and after production had been halted at Laurahütte, the manufacture of antiaircraft weapons gained special urgency, and Hanomag produced half of Germany's supply of this type of artillery. Charles was heartened by the uptick in bombings. He knew the end of his suffering was near; if he could just hold out until then.

"In spite of everything we were suffering," wrote Arthur Lehman, "our hopes were nourished again and again by the immense aircraft swarms that flew over our camp day and night. Especially at the beginning of March. The daytime alarm usually announced a bombardment of Hannover and the surrounding area when the weather was good. In the factory, our people went to special places for the shelters. [When we were] in the camp, we had to stay in the barracks. As soon as Quakernack and his men had disappeared in the shelter built especially for them – and the gentlemen were very anxious for their safety – then we workers went outside. Then came the swarms of planes – they seemed innumerable to us. One squad after another, as it seemed to us, flew over the camp. A bomb was always being dropped from a plane in each group, and we were able to follow its descent until the impact could be heard from the city." Never ones to waste an opportunity, the SS used the bomb craters around the camp to bury their victims.

Hannover and its surroundings were heavily bombed in the fall and winter of 1944-1945 with a combined effort between the two Allies: 623 planes in October, 615 in November, 495 in December, and 843 planes in January 1945. The skies were very crowded. Between the pummeling of Germany and the news that the paid Polish labor force shared with them, the prisoners knew the end was in sight for the Nazis. Meanwhile, work in the factory continued, even though the bombed-out railways held up necessary supplies. On March 28, 1945, Allied Flight Engineer, Lyman R. Huffmann, Jr., of Denison Texas, just 19 years old, wrote in his diary: "Mission No. 11: We bombed Hannover Germany, which was our secondary target. The mission was seven hours, 15 minutes long. We dropped 12 500-pound general-purpose bombs from 25,000 feet." It was one of the largest air raids on Hannover to date; the Hanomag factory was badly damaged. The leadership of Neuengamme began to plan for the inevitable evacuation orders.

In Hannover-Linden, bread was withheld from the prisoners to save for their evacuation. They would march out even more famished. During the evacuation preparations, the SS ordered a pit to be dug between the hospital barrack and the kitchen, which they claimed was to be used for air raid protection. The inmates suspected otherwise. At four meters wide and two and a half meters deep, with a water level of about 30 centimeters, the pit would offer little to no protection against an air raid attack. One SS man smugly remarked that it was to be used as a swimming pool.

In the earliest hours of April 6, 1945, American troops crossed the Weser River just 43 kilometers from Hannover in their push for Berlin. Soon after, the leaders of the Hannover subcamps received orders to evacuate in the direction of Neuengamme, "with the exception of the sick and those unable to march," wrote Arthur Lehmann. The sick would be brought to Neuengamme by train or truck. In Linden, a large wagon and two handcarts were loaded with provisions, kitchen equipment, and the Nazis' luggage. All of the office and infirmary records were burned under SS supervision.

During the final morning Appell, the prisoners lined up in the customary rows of five abreast and were told they were going on a long march. Anyone who felt unable to do so should remain in the camp; trucks would arrive to transport them later. The men did not believe the latter statement for a second. They assumed that anyone who stayed behind would be shot and thrown in the pit. "With the back and forth of people deciding if they should go or not, there was a lot of noise and confusion. Quakernack and his cronies shot a few men dead," recorded Arthur Lehmann.

Once order was restored, the men were given bread and margarine. An inmate from one of the back rows, feeling disadvantaged, pushed his way forward. Apparently, his neighbor hadn't given him any of the bread he had collected for the two of them. A riot broke out, which the trigger-happy Quakernack settled by again firing his pistol, killing the complainer instantly. He shot a few more times in the direction of the fracas for good measure. Soon, the margarine, which the men had immediately gobbled up, had unfortunate and instantaneous consequences. Since their digestive systems were unused to even a miniscule amount of fat, they soon came down with virulent diarrhea. Beginning inauspiciously with murder and dysentery, the procession formed. The SS and the guards, with their omnipresent rifles, formed a circle around the motley, feces-stained bunch, and led their prisoners out the camp gates into the tremendous destruction of Hannover.

For about three or four hours, the men who chose to remain at Hanomag stayed in their barracks. But they were starving, and the silence of the camp gave a few of them the courage to venture out. They opened the doors of their barracks and peeked out and saw... nothing. There were no guards, not even in the towers. The bravest among them went straight to the kitchen. A fight immediately broke out over the distribution of potatoes. After a while, gunshots cracked the quiet; some of the SS had come back. The prisoners tried to run for their barracks, but some of them never made it, the victims of a few SS men who were ordered to stay in the vicinity of the camp.

Oskar H., one of the men who'd elected to stay in the camp, rejected the crowded kitchen and headed instead for the SS living quarters when he heard the shots. "Me and five or six other people hid in a closet. The SS man came over and shrieked, '*Komm da raus!*' [Come out of there!] I heard someone walk out of the closet followed by a crash of the machine gun. Then I heard the SS man go from cupboard to cupboard and open [them]. When he met someone, he would shoot. Shaking with fear, I took a spoon out of my pocket and used it to push the latch down. He tried to open my closet but couldn't. Then he tried to open the bolt with the plunger [sic], but since this also failed, he probably believed that the cupboard was empty and went on."

Later, Oskar H. heard prisoners carrying the dead men out of the room. He quietly snuck out of the cupboard. "I mingled with these inmates and helped carry out the last corpse. That's how I got away. The corpses were carried into the pit that had been dug a few days earlier. The last man we brought out of the SS barracks was not yet dead. When he sat up in the pit, he was shot in the head."

Once all the adventurous inmates were either shot or contained, the SS opened the barracks doors and ordered the nervous prisoners to line up. French prisoner Georges Bonnet had fainted in the kitchen when the SS reappeared. When he regained consciousness, he could see the prisoners lined up at Appell. He surreptitiously joined the group and only then noticed he'd been shot. "At that moment, an SS man called to me, 'You! The big one! Come!' He pushed a stretcher into my hands, and with another prisoner, I was ordered to fetch the people who had been killed in the kitchen and on the potatoes. I brought them over and threw them in the pit. [Back in the kitchen], there were comrades who weren't dead yet, and among them a Belgian who said to me, 'You are French. You understand me. You can see that I'm not dead.' The SS man stood at the kitchen door and waited. I said to him, 'He's not dead.' He answered, 'I do not give a shit!' So we took him and threw him into the pit. At one corner of the pit there was a gunman in a crouched position, firing. If something moved, he would shoot. We cleaned up this whole area. Then we were ordered to search all the barracks. In one of them, we found men who were lying on the beds. The SS man ordered, 'Get up!' They got up except for one who was holding his blanket in his hands. The SS man took the blanket from him and he was covered with blood. He said, 'Come on. We'll take him with us.' I said, 'But he's not dead.' He took his revolver. Puff! He put a bullet through his head."

Could the wounded Belgian have been my father?

After the Appell, the men were ordered back to their barrack to wait for trucks to take them to a so-called 'recovery camp.' At this point, there were only about 40 original Hannover-Linden prisoners left, and they fit in one building, Barrack 2. One prisoner, Moses B., did not believe the story about the recovery camp. He decided to hide and wait for liberators. Together with his friend, Lodzi, he snuck out of the barrack and walked to Barrack 6. "We climbed up on the top bunks, loosened the lightbulbs and laid ourselves under the covers.

Then the door to our barrack was opened. There were two SS men. One tried the light switch. Then they left."

That night, Georges Bonnet found his friend, Jean. "We'd shared the same bed and had stayed together. In the kitchen, the same bullet had pierced my back and torn his stomach. Totally torn. He held his entrails in his hands. I dragged him as best I could to a bedside."

There are varying accounts about the last hours at Hannover-Linden, all from very reliable sources. According to *The Encyclopedia of Camps and Ghettos, 1933-1943*, which was published in association with the USHMM, about 110 prisoners remained at the camp when the marchers left. "A few SS officers returned with trucks to evacuate them the following day; about 50 inmates who tried to hide were shot." However, the official website of the Hannover-Linden camp specifies the deliberate, planned killing of the "prisoners incapable of marching." A plaque in the town reads: *After the camp was cleared on April 6, 1945, the SS shot 50 sick inmates [who had been] left behind.*

In postwar trials, the camp secretary, Gerhard Grande, who claimed to have witnessed the murders, testified: "On 6 April, those who couldn't walk should go to the infirmary – they would be caught up later, [the SS] said. The sick comrades were killed by a shot in the back of the neck by the returned SS guards. About 50 prisoners [had been] left in the camp because they were too sick for the long march."

The pit the prisoners were ordered to dig a few days before the evacuation also points to premeditated murders.

Early the next morning, as the SS had said, two trucks came to transport the survivors to Bergen-Belsen. "We were told that we would be leaving within ten minutes," recalled Georges Bonnet. "I picked up Jean and pushed him behind the door. I couldn't do more. I was the last to go out and held the door... But an SS man saw him and said, 'Get out!' Jean said to me, 'Georges, take me with you!' I couldn't. It was impossible. He was too heavy. I was alone. I could not. The SS man then aimed his rifle and I got Jean's brain on my feet."

Georges Bonnet later estimated that he brought about 40 bodies to the pit. Later reports estimated the figure was as high as 52. Bonnet, Oskar H., his brother, Erwin, Lokshi, and a Dutchman named Henrik deKlepper, who had survived by hiding in a chimney, were among the few survivors to give testimony regarding the last hours in the camp. In a letter to a fellow survivor dated September 6, 1945, deKlepper wrote: "Not long after our guard and [the] SS men had fled, there was a festive atmosphere in the camp. After some time, however, a group of SS men had returned and everyone was shot... All other prisoners [were] shot and it is really a miracle that I am still alive. Reverend Ringnalda and Wouter Vandenberg were shot down six feet from us as the Americans approached." The recipient of the letter commented: "DeKlepper could only have survived because he was hiding in a chimney. All prisoners were taken after the massacre [and thrown] into that big pit they themselves had to dig. Quakernack had ordered the SS men to 'put everything in order in the camp after their departure.'"

Why did the SS shoot some men who were unable to march when the next day, they trucked others to Bergen-Belsen? The survivors clearly conveyed the impression of a panic reaction on the part of the SS, generated by the sight of prisoners who saw themselves as liberated. The leader of the SS group that Quakernack had ordered to return to Hanomag reported to him that a "mutiny" had broken out among the sick prisoners. The only thing I know for certain is that my father died during his detention at Hannover-Linden. I strongly believe he was killed on April 6. My mother's story of him being killed by "firing squad," and her pronouncement that there was a survivor who returned to tell the story (deKlepper?) is too similar. Historian Rolf Keller has estimated that between 110 and 180 prisoners died in the camp between February 3 and April 6.

My father came so close to being liberated. Still, he suffered until nearly the end of the war, trying to hang on in the most horrific conditions. Hannover was liberated on April 10. Bergen-Belsen, where the Hannover prisoners were marched, was liberated on April 15. It's a bitter pill for me to swallow, even now, almost 80 years later.

34

MAJER PILA

On March 5, 1920, a baby boy was born to Chaja and Emanuel Pila in the shtetl of Zelów, Poland. One-third of the town's roughly 5,300 people were Jewish. The couple named their first-born Majer. Five more children followed roughly every other year: three boys and two girls, straining the Pila's meager finances. The large family lived in a one-room home without electricity or indoor plumbing. Those modern conveniences hadn't reached Zelów yet.

Chaja was a religious Orthodox Jew and Emanuel was more of a Zionist but the couple coexisted peacefully. All Jewish holidays were strictly observed by the family. When Majer was old enough to walk around the town by himself, his mother told him to close his eyes if he even so much as walked past a non-kosher butcher.

Because of the Sabbath laws, Jews couldn't work from the sunset of Fridays through the sunsets of Saturdays, which restricted them from working in the local factories and earning more money. Most Jewish men were uneducated, excluding the study of the Talmud, and had a hard time making a living. Nine out of ten Jewish families in Zelów were poor. Most Jewish men, including Emanuel, worked making handmade textiles for the lowest of wages. The whole family joined in the endeavor. One man could never produce enough cloth to feed a family, no matter how many contributors he had fathered. The youngest children sat at the spinning wheel winding thread on a spool. The older ones weaved the cloth. As the children grew and began to produce more, the younger kids had a chance for a little education.

Majer spent a few years at a cheder, a Jewish elementary school that taught him the basics of Judaism and the Hebrew language. "They were so strict! For example, by Thursday, if you couldn't memorize what [the rabbi] taught you for the week, he'd pick you up by the ears and you fell down on the floor."

It was difficult for a Jewish child to receive an education that was of any use outside the shtetl. "Most of the kids went to Jewish schools," said Majer. "But they didn't learn anything that would help them in the future. They only learned Yiddish. But in the long run, if you went somewhere else, the Yiddish didn't help too much because out in the world it's not that common a language that we [could] use everywhere." Outside of the shtetl, "it was very hard explaining what you wanted."

The Catholics in Zelów and throughout Poland were "raised to believe that Jewish people had something like horns... not included as human beings or people," said Majer. "This is what the parents and the school taught them. Jewish kids, when they went to [public] school, always got beat up."

Majer was 13 when Hitler came to power. "Very shortly thereafter, antisemitism received state support and was in full swing," he said. Before 1933, "People were laughing about Hitler, saying, 'He can never make it. He doesn't know what he's talking about.' Between Poland and Germany, there was not too much communication because at that time [we] didn't have the telephone and electricity. In our little town, before the war, there were only three Germans. By around 1935, there were so many Germans. We couldn't believe they were Germans. We were raised with them; they never said they were German. But from time to time these people just disappeared. They went to Germany to start learning Hitler's system. When they came back, they were a lot worse. They beat lots of Jews in the street. They pulled [the men's] beards out; they hit them; they killed them," he recalled.

"In 1938 we started thinking that it wasn't a joke whatever Hitler was doing." From March 11 to March 13, 1938, when German troops invaded Austria and incorporated the country into the German Reich, the Jews knew how serious Hitler was. On September 30, 1938, Germany, Italy, Great Britain, and France signed the Munich Agreement, by which Czechoslovakia was forced to surrender its border regions (the so-called Sudetenland) to Nazi Germany. German troops occupied these regions between October 1 and 10, 1938. Hitler had threatened to unleash a European war unless the Sudetenland, which contained an ethnic German majority, was surrendered to Germany. "Jewish newspapers had pictures of *Kristallnacht* [Night of Broken Glass]. We saw it was not a joke. We felt that there was a time coming when the antisemitism in Poland was going to be much, much worse than it was for my father and my grandfather," said Majer.

Most Jews in Poland, including Majer's family, were too poor to emigrate. They soothed themselves with self-talk that God would protect them. The Nazis marched into Zelów on September 6, 1939, just five days after invading Poland, and made quick work of confiscating Jewish workshops and goods. Majer was 19 years old and working as a textiles weaver, and most likely still living and working in the family home. "Right away, the Jewish people had to go into a ghetto. If you were living on a main street, you had to move to a back street," he said. "If a window faced the main street, it had to be taped. You couldn't see anything. It was restricted."

Majer's family was forced to move to the worst area of Zelów, adjacent to the garbage and sewage dump. "Nasty, dank, a lot of misery." Many Jews arrived from surrounding towns, including nearby Szczerców, my mother's birthplace. Most came with almost nothing, so the Nazi-established a *Judenrat*, a Jewish municipal administration, tasked with arranging their accommodations. Strangers were forced to live together in very tight quarters.

The Nazis soon implemented a series of anti-Jewish laws. "Jewish people could not go in the streets except for maybe an hour or two hours. Each Jew had to wear a yellow star – one on the front, one on the back. Our citizenship papers were taken away. Then the Jewish people could not buy any food and we lost the right to work."

The Judenrat was tasked with ensuring that all Nazi orders and regulations were carried out. Its members also sought to provide basic community services for the ghettoized Jews. Since they were banned from procuring food, "A kitchen was installed in the ghetto. In no way could you get out. You had to come to the kitchen with whatever you had – a bucket or whatever – to get the food. However much food you got, you couldn't complain. It wasn't food from which you could get any nourishment. They called it soup but it was plain water. And a piece of bread a day. Mother had to struggle to get each one of us a piece. It was not enough food, and you cannot call it food." The kitchen was run by the Judenrat, whom the Nazis had told exactly how much food they could dole out. Families of ten received the same amount as families of fifteen. "Most days Father didn't eat; Mother didn't eat. They gave it to the kids," said Majer in his postwar testimony.

Other Judenrat-enforced measures included the implementation of forced labor, such as cleaning the streets and collecting scrap metal, and ordering Jews to remove their hats when encountering Germans. Failure to obey any of the rules could result in the death penalty, but more often earned a severe beating.

Majer referred to the next anti-Jewish measures as "the worst of the worst. They started burning Jewish literature, Polish literature. They used the synagogues as stables for horses, cows. Then they sent the Jewish people to the Łódź ghetto or a concentration camp. They started beating, slaughtering. Plain slaughtering! They pulled out the beards. They took the rabbi and set him up on a stepladder to make shame of the Jewish religion – made him put on everything that is necessary to make the Jewish prayers [*Tallit* and *Tefillin*]. Then they would make two Jews beat him."

35

FORCED LABOR

Beginning in early 1940, the Nazis tasked the *Judenrat* with the gut-wrenching job of furnishing lists of hundreds of able-bodied Jewish men for transport to some of the 20 labor camps in the Poznań (Posen in German) region in western central Poland. Majer, young and strong, was arrested by the SS on February 15, 1940. If he had been arrested at his home, it meant his name had been intentionally placed on the list by a member of the *Judenrat* who may have known him and judged him fit for labor due to his youth. The SS also nabbed men in random street roundups.

The first Jewish labor camp in Posen began operating in the spring of 1941. At any given time, it enslaved approximately 1,000 Jews who were forced to work on public works and transportation projects, and in construction and agriculture throughout the city. Many of them endured sleeping outdoors in the worst of conditions. The men were abused, starved, and many became sick. In his post-war testimony, Majer never discussed his time as a forced laborer. After an unknown period of time, he was released back to Zelów. In the volume, *The Chronicle of the Łódź Ghetto 1941–1944*, a daily record listing the main events in Poland's second largest ghetto to Warsaw, there is a chart for the beginning of every month entitled, *Population Changes in the Month*. The lists are headed: "Births; Deaths; Arrivals; To Prison; To Manual Labor; and Returned from Manual Labor." It made logistical sense for the Nazis to return the laborers to their homes. That way they could deport whole families to the extermination camps together, making for easier record keeping.

When Majer returned from Poznań, he periodically left the ghetto as part of a street-sweeping crew guarded by *Volksdeutschen*, ethnic Germans who living in area. "We knew them," remembered Majer incredulously. "We were living with them all those years." The streets didn't necessarily need sweeping. The work was meant to "humiliate you and keep you as a slave," he said. "You just feel like a vegetable."

I made a shocking discovery when I read Majer's camp records for the first time. Between the end of his forced labor and his deportation from the ghetto, he married a girl named Natia. His marriage status was recorded in his concentration camp file. On a form next to *Name der Ehefrau* [name of wife] is written *Natia geb Pila*. *Geb* is an abbreviation of the word *geboren*, the German word for 'born'. In other words, Natia's maiden name was Pila. Majer explained in his testimony, "In Poland, nobody married people from other families. They married no one else around except in the family—cousin to cousin, cousin to cousin, cousin to cousin—and this built up the family. And it was not just in my town. In *every* town!" Majer never told me he had been married before the war. I don't know if my mother even knew. He also never mentioned losing a wife in his testimony. Many survivors who lost a spouse and/or children found it too painful to talk about. Sadly, there is not a single surviving record of Natia Pila neé Pila. It's as if she never existed. The Nazis destroyed every document pertaining to the Jewish community of Zelów, including the marriage license of Majer and Natia Pila.

On June 14, 1942, a number of Zelów's Jews were deported to the Chełmno extermination camp, but 96 of them, including Majer, were sent to the Łódź ghetto. After spending only one night there, Majer was sent away at 8:30 the next morning with almost 300 other men from Zelów and Bełchatów. This dovetails with Majer's testimony that he was only in the Łódź ghetto for one day.

Majer never saw Natia again.

36

MORE FORCED LABOR

Majer's first concentration camp record is from Auschwitz; he arrived on August 27, 1943 from the labor camp Wollstein/Wolsztyn. The weighty volume, *Auschwitz Chronicle*, a daily compendium of happenings at the camp much like the book about the Łódź Ghetto, states: "One thousand twenty-six Jews were transported from the labor camp in Wolsztyn in the Poznań *voivodeship* [administrative district] to KL [*Konzentrationslager*] Auschwitz. Ten people were killed in the gas chamber, and the remaining 1,016 men were sent to the camp with the numbers 140721 – 141736. Among them were Jews of Polish origin."

There is very little information on Wollstein, and Majer didn't mention it in his testimony. A search of the Arolsen Archives, produced only one document, a list of seven simple questions and seven very simple (some only one word) answers. Still, finding it was a watershed moment in learning more about Majer's wartime footprints.

Wollstein was one of 20 subcamps in the Poznán area. Some forced laborers helped build Germany's famous *Autobahn* highway.

Wollstein didn't open until March 1943. Majer was one of 120 Jewish inmates who worked broadening a river for the village of Liechtenstein (not to be confused with the tiny country of the same name). Prisoners were guarded by the Gestapo and wore civilian clothing. Majer was there for just five months before he was deported to Auschwitz on August 26, 1943.

Majer's Auschwitz tattoo number, 141449, verifies that he was on the transport mentioned in the *Auschwitz Chronicle*. With him were his cousins Josef Pila, Berek Pila, and Abram Pila, demonstrating that they must have been arrested together in Łódź. The large extended family had most likely been living together in a single cramped room in the ghetto. Tattoo number 141450 went to Josef; 141452 to Berek; 141453 to Abram. There was no information about whoever received the number between Josef and Berek.

There are nine months between Majer's arrest in June 1942 to the opening of Wollstein in March 1943 for which I have no information. One survivor who was deported to Auschwitz with Majer discussed in detail two other Posen-area camps where he had been a slave laborer, but he never mentioned Wollstein.

37

MAJER IN BIRKENAU

"The human being is strong," Majer responded when asked to recall his journey to Auschwitz. "We were pushed into the cattle train. If 50 people could go in, there were maybe 100, 150, pressed together like herring. Standing up. If you wanted to sit down, you must sit down on the people. Open cars. Lots of people die right away. They didn't even take them off. They left them laying until we reached Auschwitz."

He continued: "The only thing that we did know was that there was no way to come back. This was on our mind already. We saw and felt it, that we were going to a place where we were going to get burned or killed, and we are not going to come back anymore. This was the feeling." Majer envied those who died in the cattle cars. "They are lucky. They are dead. I hope the next day I'll be dead!" He explained: "We didn't want to go through what we were looking forward to. We were not going to a place where we were coming back from anyway, so why should we use the time and be miserable?" In other words, Majer knew from the way he'd been treated as a forced laborer and from rumors he had heard, that if his life was spared at Selektion, existence in the camp would be worse than death.

One thought kept running through his mind during the long trip to Auschwitz. "I hope I don't get to see a brother suffering the way I suffer. Please, let me not see how my father is suffering! This was the most important thing because [I wouldn't be able to] help him. Whatever was going to happen, let him not be in my place where I am. We were so close – between one brother and the other one. It would be impossible. One word: Impossible!"

When his train arrived, he said, "We were very weak. The Germans opened the locked doors and started screaming and beating: 'Raus! Raus! Raus! Raus!' [Out! Out! Out! Out!] Left! Right! Left! Right!" Two lines were quickly formed. "We didn't know which line is good and which line is bad." Majer's life, contrary to his wish, was spared. He was chosen for labor and registered in the camp: stripped, showered, deloused, shaved, tattooed. His new name was 141449. "I wouldn't say [the tattoo] was sore or hurt. At this time I didn't feel anything anyway. A human being is so strong. In painful times he gets stronger. You're having no fever; you're having no pain – you know why? Because everything is dead in you! For example, if you have a pain in the arm, the arm is dead. If you have pain in the stomach, it's dead. It changes your whole system from a human being to just nothing."

The typical Birkenau quarantine period was three weeks, but after only eight days, Majer was chosen for labor in a subcamp. Despite his short stay, the Nazis completed a lengthy registration form for him, annotating everything from his birthdate, place of birth, last address, occupation, the names of his parents and his wife (the only surviving evidence of Natia) to detailed descriptions of his facial attributes. The form had an entire section devoted to descriptions of his nose, mouth, ears, facial shape, facial hair, hair color, and the quality of his teeth. Obviously, registration occurred before he was physically processed, since the presence of any hair would have been noted before he'd been shaved. The queer notations describing his features were used in the Nazis' pseudoscientific racial studies.

Majer's features were described as such:

Nose: "expanded"
Mouth: "thick-lipped"
Face: "oval"
Ears: "large"
Beard: "None"
Eyes: "Gray"
Hair: "Black"
Teeth: "Good, five missing teeth"

In Nazi propaganda posters, meant to stir fear and revulsion among Gentiles, the typical Jew was portrayed with an enormous, hooked nose and lips grossly out of proportion with the rest of the face. In other words, "thick-lipped" Majer, with his "expanded" nose and black hair met the criteria of a grotesque, non-Aryan, inferior Jew.

38

MAJER IN JANINA

Eighteen kilometers from Birkenau, in a town called Libiąż, there was a large coal mine called Janina. IG Farben, the German chemical and pharmaceutical conglomerate, had acquired a majority share of Janina in March 1943 so it could supply coal to a chemical factory it owned near Auschwitz. Subsequently, a camp for British POWs was established at Janina so the men could be forced laborers in the mine. But the British prisoners caused problems of sabotage and refusals to work, so their output was deemed inefficient. Had they been Jews, they would have been immediately shot for their defiance.

IG Farben desperately needed large amounts of coal to run the chemical company, so they negotiated with Rudolf Höss, the commandant of Auschwitz, to source prisoner labor from the camp. After an inspection by Höss and a representative of IG Farben, they agreed that the POWs would be replaced by camp prisoners. IG Farben requested 300, twice the number of POWs. They also requested that Janina's infrastructure be expanded to accommodate 900 prisoners by the end of 1943.

In a letter to Höss dated September 4, 1943, the Auschwitz camp doctor wrote: "For the Kommando 'Janina' certain prisoners were today released from camp, examined, and found healthy and fit for work. The prisoners and their clothing were deloused. They are equipped with proper clothing. Before giving accommodations at the arrivals desk, their clothes and laundry must be deloused again. The prisoners have not been through any quarantine here and have to be placed in one at their destination for four weeks from arrival. During the quarantine period, they must not come into contact with the civilization population."

"My uniform was blue and white stripes," recalled Majer. "We didn't get any underwear, we didn't get an undershirt. Wooden shoes. These were our clothes forever and ever. You had to be very careful. If somebody steals your clothes or your shoes, you're not getting back any. You're shot."

Subcamp Janinagrube [*Grube* is German for pit] officially opened the day the first 300 prisoners arrived from Birkenau. The director of the subcamp was *Unterscharführer* [junior squad leader] Franz Baumgartner, who was remembered by survivors as not especially violent, though there was an instance in the winter of 1943-1944 when he ordered ten prisoners to stand naked next to an electrified, barbed wire fence until they died from exposure.

About 250 of the new inmates were the Polish Jews who'd been transported to Auschwitz on August 27-28 with Majer. Once their quarantine ended they were assigned to work underground in the mine. The other 50 prisoners were professional bricklayers, carpenters, and metal workers, who went to work immediately to expand the subcamp. They built a fence, new prisoner barracks, and quarters for the SS. After the infrastructure was finished, almost all of the prisoners were sent to work in the mine.

Janina was surrounded by a double row of barbed wire hung from concrete posts. The outer fence was electrified. In the corners of the camp stood four wooden guard towers equipped with floodlights. Over the gate there was the inscription *Arbeitslager Janinagrube* [Janinagrube Labor Camp]. Some of the prisoners were housed in one of the existing brick buildings formerly used to house mine employees. Detention cells were in the basement of the building. The remaining prisoners lived in wooden huts and slept in two-tiered wooden bunks. One of the barracks in the middle of the camp housed the hospital. There was also a kitchen, baths, and latrines.

The hygienic conditions in Janina were grossly inadequate. There was no heat or hot water until the fall of 1944; after a backbreaking day in the cold, wet mine, the prisoners, thickly dusted in black coal, had to wash in frigid water and redress in the same wet, filthy clothes. It was only after the intervention of the mine management that a shower with warm water was installed in the camp washroom and central heating added to the prisoner barracks. After this, the men were cleaner when they redressed in their filthy, wet uniforms.

As grungy as the uniforms were, "Most of us slept in our clothing and shoes," said Majer. "People would steal them from each other. When your shoes got stolen it was very, very bad and it took a long, long time to replace them. You would take rags and wrap them around under your legs. It could be snow or it could be heat or it could be rain. There were no facilities for being treated like a human being."

In between the barracks was an open space used for the dreaded Appells, which the SS used to further abuse the prisoners. The coal mine operated in three eight-hour shifts, beginning at 6 a.m. However, "If you went to work [at 6 a.m.] they took us out maybe at 3 in the afternoon, and they were keeping us in line for maybe two hours. God forgive if one did escape! Counting and counting and counting. They ran up the time."

Appell was repeated in the evening. The SS often harassed the prisoners for two or three hours, not only in making them stand but in ordering them to perform penal exercises such as frog jumps. At other times, they were made to perform various types of work in the camp, such as carrying bricks or poles. "When we came home at 9 in the night, this was still not the end of the day," said Majer. "We were thinking we were going to sleep but this was not the case. Then they came in [to the barracks] and beat us and ran us outside to unload trains for the Germans. So we had no time to keep ourselves clean even if we wanted to."

As in Birkenau, the Appell was also an opportunity for the SS to perform Selektions. "We did the best we could for somebody who was weak, to hold them up. Maybe later they were going to get stronger and live through this period. But very, very rarely did they live. When one was too weak to get up, the Germans were all over [him]. Most of these people were shot right away."

After morning Appell, the prisoners were handed their bread, which Majer always ate right away since, "Nobody could steal from my stomach. Food was the most important thing if you wanted to survive." Then the men marched to the mine. The labor was grueling. Prisoners often stood up to their waists in water or, as Majer testified, lay on their stomachs to dig out the coal: "We didn't have proper clothes. Before you got to the coal, the wet stones were dripping. Until you got all the way through to the coal, miles and miles, it dripped. Most prisoners got sick. The only thing that allowed you to survive a little bit and not get pneumonia was to get an empty cement sack and just cover up. You could put a double sack around your legs to keep the water out," he said. "We came home at night and they poured what they called food. It was plain water. They put in some leaves. I don't know what it was. It wasn't enough to live on. There were no plates, no knives. You just had a can, and you hoped that nobody had stolen it. You couldn't get another one. When you were very hungry and weak, people started pushing one another to get to the soup. The punishment they gave us was that they took away the privilege of eating the soup. You didn't get anything to eat until the next morning."

The lack of nourishment, enduring claustrophobic postures for hours underground, the constant damp, and the poor air quality in the mine caused the prisoners' strength to fail quickly. The average life expectancy at Janina was four to six weeks. Many prisoners suffered a variety of fractures and internal injuries, as well as illnesses such as swelling from starvation, tuberculosis, typhus, scurvy, and respiratory illnesses. And there was always the physical abuse of the SS. Selektions in the camp hospital were frequent, and in the prisoners' opinions, as good as death sentences. The condemned were trucked to Birkenau to be gassed. Knowing this, many severely injured prisoners continued to work, hiding their injuries from the guards. Once a week a truck arrived from Auschwitz to deliver supplies and to pick up the steady supply of corpses stored in the cellar in a specially designed chest next to the detention cells. When temperatures rose, the bodies were sprinkled with chlorine to prevent putrefaction.

In March 1944, Unterscharführer Baumgartner was replaced by Oberscharführer Hermann Kleemann, promoted from his position as warehouse manager. Like Walter Quakernack, Kleemann was sadistically violent and often drunk. He was quickly nicknamed "Revolver King" by the prisoners because he resorted to shooting so quickly. His pistol pouch was always open. Several prisoners recalled his love for a game in which he'd make inmates hold playing cards so he could partake in target practice. He often missed. If he struck the inmates' hands, injuring them badly enough so they couldn't work, they were sent to the gas chambers. Unfortunately, he was not a good shot. Kleemann also enjoyed organizing boxing matches between the prisoners and the mine management, growing excited "when the blood flowed," recalled one survivor.

Despite the poor odds, Majer lasted almost a year in Janina before falling ill with pneumonia. There is a camp record of his hospital stay at Auschwitz III-Monowitz in July 1944. He must have been desperately ill to go, knowing how prone the SS were to hospital

Selektions. But he recovered, transferring back to Birkenau, which ironically contributed to saving his life.

"I came to Birkenau paralyzed on one side of my body because of the water dripping. I think it was the right side that was paralyzed a little bit. And I couldn't go to work." Majer knew the implications of not working. "But I was lucky. This guy who was in charge of the [Block], he had a little bit of – I don't know – feelings. I didn't go out to work for maybe six or seven months."[1] "He let me do work like sweeping in the room only, and that was all. Slowly my health came back – slowly."

Majer managed to remain free of illness, unlike many prisoners. "Typhus and dysentery came mostly when people weren't careful and ate garbage," Majer explained. "You had to watch what you ate. You could stay away from trouble by eating a little bit of soup, a piece of bread. A person could survive on very little food if you didn't get into trouble and get a sickness – you get used to it."

---

1. This is undoubtedly an exaggeration, though it may have seemed that long.

39

MAJER'S LAST DAYS IN BIRKENAU AND THE DEATH MARCH

On January 17, 1945, as Red Army units advanced on the outlying areas of Kraków, a strong Russian air attack on the retreating Germans ensued. In Auschwitz I and Birkenau, 31,060 prisoners were lined up for for their last Appell. A few subcamps were already evacuating, but Birkenau registered the unfortunate Engelbert Marketsch, its last prisoner, who had been freshly transferred from Mauthausen. He received number 202499.

Late that evening, the inmates of Birkenau and most of its subcamps were told to prepare for evacuation. Majer did not give many details of his evacuation experience. A survivor named Freddie Knoller wrote in his memoir, *Desperate Journey*: "That night was bitterly cold. I could not sleep for the possibilities which plagued me, possibilities of death on the one hand, and escape and liberation on the other." Survivor Pierre Berg recalled: "Rumors circulated that we were headed to the town of Gleiwitz. No one knew exactly how far that was, but it became increasingly apparent that we would be walking all night."

In the early hours of January 18, the prisoners received extra rations of bread and soup. Told they could bring their blankets with them, they lined up in a seemingly endless ribbon and the process of clearing 56,000 fragile prisoners commenced. Columns of people left Birkenau at specific intervals in temperatures of –20 °C/ –4 °F. Most of them, like Majer, wore only their striped prison uniforms and wooden clogs; some were barefooted, while others had rags tied around their feet. "The snow was becoming deeper, filling my wooden shoes and turning my feet into icicles," wrote Pierre Berg. "I feared frostbite wouldn't be far off. Our ranks began to break as Muselmänner struggled to plow through snowdrifts. The gusts became more violent, causing my eyes to water and burn, and it seemed nearly impossible to get the frigid air into my heaving lungs. The wind lifted the snow in eddies, covering the tracks of the men in front of me. I tripped over an unexpected obstacle – a man's body covered by a thin blanket of snow. A few moments later I came upon another body, this one with an SS bullet in his neck. Walking further, I realized that the dead were forming a steady line along the side of the road."

"We were just glued together," wrote Freddie Knoller. "When you got behind the line, they would shoot you. They would shoot you if you laid down. There were no beatings; they shot us."

The evacuees advanced along two main routes. Majer's march stretched 55 kilometers from Birkenau to the northwest as far as Gleiwitz. He was already exhausted by the trek from Janina to Birkenau.

Pierre Berg wrote: "We slipped through the darkened town of Auschwitz and I caught a glimpse of town folk watching us through the cracks in their closed shutters. When we reached the country road, walking became even harder because the surface was frozen. It started snowing and icy winds whipped our faces while clumps of mud-stained snow dragged at our feet. A prisoner in the column ahead of mine slipped and fell and seemed unable to get up. An SS man at once dispatched him with a bullet through the head and some prisoners were ordered to throw the body into a ditch," recalled Pierre Berg. "We came upon empty villages abandoned before the Russians' advance, and all the while the distant rumbling artillery of their heavy guns accompanied us. We dragged ourselves like automatons through one after another of these villages, each [of us] seeming to hold out slender hope that we might be permitted to stop, perhaps to even get a little nourishment. They marched us until daybreak," he continued. "Then they herded us into a bombed-out tileworks that had a perimeter fence that was still intact. I collapsed on a pile of bricks and pulled my blanket over my head. Fearing I would freeze to death, my sleep was fitful at best. A couple of hours later, the SS called for assembly. My legs were painfully stiff and heavy when I stood. How many more miles could they handle?"

As the marchers were formed in columns of ten-back, five-across, they grabbed handfuls of snow to stanch their thirst. Majer testified: "You might find a piece of ice and chew it. There was no food. None at all. There was a little bit of snow. You made a ball, and you'd chew it a little bit – ice – no food at all. And they didn't need to beat us. They shot us. We were just glued together, and we marched one after another. When you got behind the line they would shoot you. They would shoot you if you laid down."

When the marchers finally reached Gleiwitz, the SS put them in a brick factory to rest for a few hours. It felt like they had just gone to sleep when angry screams of "Raus!" woke them. After re-forming into columns, they finally received hot soup and bread. The SS men went back into the brick factory to shoot the people who hadn't stirred, making sure they were truly dead. Finally, the weary group was marched to the railway station and loaded onto open cattle wagons.

Zygfryd Halbreich marched with Freddie and Majer. He said, "On the evening of January 21, 1945, we were divided into two transports, one directed to KZ Buchenwald. The second transport [containing Halbreich, Knoller, Berg, and Majer] was directed to Mauthausen, and from there, because of overcrowding in the camp, we were directed to KZ [Dora-]Mittelbau. The loading took about three to four hours. We were traveling in open freight wagons, in which there were between 80 and 120 people."

"We were squeezed in so tightly we were hardly able to sit," said Freddie Knoller. "It started to snow again. We each had our blanket and we pulled them over our heads. I do not remember how many days and nights we traveled. We sucked snow to quench our thirst. Many continued to die, and to make more room we piled their bodies at one end where they stank horribly." There was one benefit to the exposure. "We thanked God that we were in open wagons so that some of the stench of excrement and death was carried away in the bitterly cold air."

Four days later, having received no food, the prisoners arrived at Mauthausen in the early morning hours. After just an hour's stop at the train station, though, the transport was sent on its way; Mauthausen was too overcrowded. The prisoners would not be fed until the train reached a camp that could take them. After enduring three more days, they arrived at Nordhausen/Mittelbau-Dora. Dora-Mittelbau, also called Dora-Nordhausen, or simply Dora or Nordhausen, was in central Germany near the southern Harz Mountains, north of the town of Nordhausen. Thankfully, it was only a ten-minute walk from the train station to the camp.

Five hundred out of the original 4,000 from Gleiwitz perished. The surviving prisoners were in such poor physical condition that another 600 people died in the first two days.

Approximately 9,000-15,000 marchers died or were murdered during the evacuation from the Auschwitz camp system. In addition to speaking very little of the misery he endured throughout his ten-day evacuation, Majer, also skipped over his time as a slave laborer in Dora-Mittelbau. If not for the testimony of others who were with him, I would have no knowledge of the inhumanity he endured and witnessed there.

40

MITTELBAU-DORA

As soon as the train came to a stop, the wagons were immediately surrounded by SS men. "They flung open the doors and backed away as the odor [of us] engulfed them," wrote Freddie Knoller. "We could scarcely stand, though the SS soon recovered their shouting voices and used whips and blows to drive us once more from the wagons. The rows of five we now stood in were far fewer; it seemed to me that more than half of us had died on the journey. We were led to a building where we were ordered to strip, and then taken to a long, enclosed room with hundreds of shower heads...I was beyond caring whether this chamber would be the place of my end or not, but when the showers hissed, it was water, hot water, which splashed down on us. Evidently the Nazis had further use for us." Indeed they did.

Any cleansing benefits from the all-too-brief hot water disappeared after the men were forced to put the putrid uniforms they had worn out of Auschwitz back on. Majer was officially registered, rebranded 108432. When he arrived at his new barrack, he was pleasantly surprised to find it heated. The unaccustomed comfort and some soup and bread boosted the morale of the men considerably. The next morning, they even received a slice of salami with their ersatz coffee and bread, another unanticipated treat. Things were looking up. "Most of the prisoners I saw looked reasonably well," wrote Freddie Knoller. "There were no Kapos here."

Dora-Mittelbau had begun as a satellite camp of Buchenwald, when 107 of its prisoners were trucked in during the late summer of 1943. In October 1944, it became an independent camp with its own administration and forty subcamps. Forced laborers were tasked with digging out deep tunnels in the surrounding mountains in an effort to move German arms production underground, where it would be sheltered from increasingly heavy Allied air raids. At the camp's inception, inmates were often housed inside the cold, damp tunnels for long periods of time without daylight or adequate sanitation. When the factory became fully functioning, barracks were built outside of the tunnel system.

In his memoir, *Scheisshaus Luck*, Pierre Berg gave a description of the herculean task of building the tunnels. "As the days went by I realized how enormous and elaborate the underground plant was. The two main tunnels, which were about a mile long, worked as assembly lines fed by a total of 46 transverse tunnel workshops. If the top of the Kohnstein hill were shaved off, the plant would look like a ladder."

On February 1, 1945, Richard Baer, a former commandant of Auschwitz, became the new commandant of Mittelbau. The evacuation of Auschwitz had left many hardened SS officers without posts and Baer promptly installed them throughout his new camp, increasing the brutality and the rate of executions. Because of the harsh conditions, 16-hour labor shifts, and the brutality of the SS, Mittelbau-Dora had one of the highest mortality rates of any concentration camp within Germany.

Mittelbau-Dora became the main production factory of the infamous V1 and V-2 (Vengeance) rockets: long-range missiles that were launched on London from the coast of France. Hitler hoped these new weapons would turn the tide of war in Germany's favor. The V-1 rockets carried 250 kilograms of explosives, but they weren't effective because their accuracy depended solely on the direction and speed of the wind, making them easy targets for fast fighter planes. The V-2 rockets were a different matter. These long-range missiles, with the capacity to fly at twice the speed of sound, had guidance systems and carried over 900 kilograms of explosives.

Pierre Berg viewed the rockets' delicate instrumentation as easy sabotage. "The slightest shock would render the precision instruments I installed in the electric circuits useless, and I saw to it that they got it good." He wasn't the only laborer involved in resisting the Nazis. One prisoner was, unfortunately, caught urinating on some machinery in the tunnel. He was ordered to drop his pants and bend over a trestle, to which he was bound hand and foot. Then an SS man beat him 25 times with a truncheon in front of the other prisoners. Mittelbau survivor, Ya'acov Handeli testified: "Many tried to sabotage [their work] by putting sand in the rockets. When the Nazis caught them, they took 50 Jews and hung them slowly so they were strangled to death. It took them 15 to 20 minutes to die. They made all the prisoners watch. They told us, 'If we catch you, you will all die like this.'" Freddie Knoller also recorded the mass hanging in his book. "Short ropes were placed around the workers' necks. The [same] electrical mechanism used to lift heavy parts of rockets was activated, which lifted the hooks slowly from the ground. We had to watch..."

This murderous spectacle also left quite an impression on Pierre Berg. "One day the SS discovered sabotage in one of the shops. They didn't bother with an investigation. They simply hung the whole, Kapo and all. Fifty men were tethered to a rail that was then hoisted into the air by a crane used to lift the V-2s. They were left hanging near the tunnel entrance as a reminder to us to be good little slaves.

Passing before those dangling bodies – that row of purple faces with protruding eyes and tongues – didn't deter me from my sabotage. It just gave me more fuel to be relentless in my mission."

As the weeks passed, the SS seemed increasingly nervous. The prisoners could hear the nearby boom of artillery fire. Simultaneously, conditions at Mittelbau began to worsen; prisoners were only fed sporadically. One day they might receive an extra ration, the next day, nothing. The soup became increasingly watery with no real nutritional value. Treats such as margarine and sausage stopped completely. "The whole system was collapsing around us," said Freddie Knoller.

"With the Allies rolling farther into Germany," wrote Pierre Berg, "not a day passed without an air raid. Nordhausen was constantly encircled in a red halo. The fire brigades were no match for the firestorms caused by the bombings. The civilian workers would come into the tunnel coated with black soot and dust, and you could see the demoralization in their eyes. I could also see it in the eyes of the SS and, as in Auschwitz when the Red Army was edging closer, our fate became my overriding fear. Soon there would be no place the Nazis could keep us. Were they planning to kill us all, eradicate the witnesses to what had to be the crime of the century? Or would we wake up one morning to find that they had stole [sic] away in the night?"

At least 1,700 V-2 and over 6,000 V-1 rockets were built from January to early April 1945. This figure is astonishing considering that in March, 16,000 prisoners from camps in the east had been added to the population all at once. The death rate in Mittelbau's last month was very high: 5,000 prisoners perished in the weeks before its evacuation. The overcrowding had reached terrifying proportions. The camp had a capacity for 14,000 inmates but in early spring 1945 there were nearly 21,000.

In late March a desperate Hitler, just one month before his suicide, ordered the production of a new jet aircraft at Mittelbau, the Messerschmidt Me-262. This was to be Germany's final chance to alter the war's course by undermining the total supremacy of the British and American air forces. Reich Minister of Propaganda Josef Goebbels boasted that the Me-262 would enable "clearing our skies again." Hans Kammler, the Nazi in charge of the most important military production lines in the armaments system – the Messerschmidts and the V-rockets – was loath to abandon the sophisticated production project at Mittelbau and leave it to the Americans. As far as he was concerned, every possible effort must be made to transfer the prisoners and the production lines to a place where they could still be exploited. Hitler, too, had given explicit orders that under no circumstances was equipment or the means of assisting the enemy in their war against Germany permitted to fall into enemy hands. That order and Kammler's single-minded determination to continue producing at least part of the sophisticated weaponry at a site that the fighting had not yet reached motivated the large-scale evacuation of Dora-Mittelbau.

For two days beginning on April 3, Mittelbau was attacked in two waves by several hundred Allied bombers. According to Pierre Berg, as one fighter plane strafed the entrance to the tunnel, he could see the pilot as the plane zipped by. "Our guards hit the ground. The pilot looped back, and in a steep dive, dropped the bomb strapped to the belly of his plane. It exploded on the tracks between the entrance and the train. The Nazis stayed prone with their hands clasped over their heads and their weapons lying next to them and the plane circled above us like a hawk. I looked at the cowards and thought how easy it would be to overwhelm them if a few of us would just grab their guns." Approximately 75 percent of the town was destroyed. Out of 40,000 inhabitants, roughly 8,800 people were killed and 20,000 lost their homes.

Commandant Baer received formal orders on April 4 to immediately begin evacuation procedures. In a great hurry and with the utmost of brutality, the Auschwitz-trained guards drove the inmates into cattle cars once again. By this time, the prisoners were so ill that 1,100 of them died the next day. By the end of April 6, almost all the prisoners from the main camp and the subcamps were evacuated. The last transport to leave the main camp, consisting of 4,000 prisoners, departed on April 5 at about 9 p.m. They were loaded onto approximately 90 open freight cars, accompanied by about 50 armed SS guards. The train traveled in a northerly direction for four days until it was forced to stop in Münchehofe due to the advancing US forces. The convoy turned south.

Although Majer didn't speak of his second evacuation, Freddie Knoller did. "A short while into our journey we stopped, the scream of sirens announcing an air raid. Then we journeyed on, hearing the retreating drone of planes overhead. Now, with the temporary distraction of this incident removed, thirst returned to plague us again. And once more death and excrement began to fill the wagon. At one point in the night the doors rolled back and we received soup and bread. Once in a while we stopped for meager refreshment at a village, where the local inhabitants seemed unsurprised to see these skeletons in striped pajamas. We were five days on that wagon before we finally arrived at Bergen-Belsen. The camp, about 60 kilometers northeast of Hannover, was vast and crammed full. My group was put into a brick barrack used by soldiers. Other prisoners were put into the usual wooden buildings."

At least 85,000 prisoners were transported to Bergen-Belsen as the concentration camps near the front lines were evacuated. Only a minority of the Dora-Mittelbau inmates, some 7,400 out of 23,700, followed a direct route from the camp to their destination. Most of the transports roamed the highways, suffering endless delays, mishaps, and transportation shortages.

When the American forces entered Dora-Mittelbau on April 11, 1945, they found about 100 sick prisoners left behind at the subcamp, Boelcke.[1] Many of them lived for only a few days after liberation. According to a report published by the Americans a few days later, 2,000 corpses were counted at the site.

---

1. The main camp and the other subcamps had been almost entirely evacuated.

41

LIBERATION

"Nobody knew what was happening or where they were," recalled Majer of his arrival at Bergen-Belsen. "We were very weak. I weighed only 60 pounds. Everybody had the same look. We were all laying down. We didn't do any more work. The Gestapo had already put white ribbons on their arms – they were ready to give up. They called themselves *Lagerists* [storehouse clerks]. They were just looking after the camp, but they didn't get any more orders. We were just laying down. That's all. We didn't know what would happen."

Survivor Violette Fintz was evacuated to Bergen-Belsen about a month before Majer. "Belsen was in the beginning bearable and we had bunks to sleep on and a small ration of soup and bread. But as the camp got fuller, our group and many others were given a barrack to hold about 700 lying on the floor without blankets and without food or anything. It was a pitiful scene as the camp was attacked by lice and most of the people had typhus and cholera. I went out of the block to try and find some water. It is impossible for me to express the scene that was before me: piles of bodies already decomposing, in fact about a mile of bodies." She continued, "Many people talk about Auschwitz, it was a horrible camp; but Belsen, no words can describe it. There was no need to work as we were just put there with no food, no water, no anything, eaten by lice."

Freddie Knoller wrote: "There was no running water in the latrines because they were blocked and overflowing, the smell of excrement filled the entire camp. The water in the washrooms was polluted. The only drinkable water was from a solitary tap in what was the kitchen area, where you had to stand for several hours to obtain a cup. We were now, in truth, less than human."

Ya'acov Handeli recounted a grotesque story: "We were so hungry. I dug into the ground trying to find roots to eat. The ground was full of dead people. Some people found sharp stones and cut flesh from the freshly dead and roasted it over a fire and ate it. Cannibalism was rampant."

Majer remembered the day he was freed. "One day we saw a tank with the Star of David on it," he said. "Later on we found out that it was the Jewish Brigade of the British Army. They came to Bergen-Belsen and they did the best they could for us, but there was no food – nothing but liberation. We saw this one tank, and then another tank, and we couldn't believe it."

The British 11th Armored Division liberated Bergen-Belsen on April 15, 1945. A jeep entered the camp, followed by a truck carrying a loudspeaker playing in many different languages: "My dear friends! You are liberated by the Allied Forces!"

Survivor Alan Zimm recalled: "Everyone was crying. It was such an emotional experience. People were jumping and hugging and kissing. Everyone was running to the jeep. Military Police (MPs) came down from their vehicles and people were lifting them on their shoulders."

But few former prisoners still possessed the energy to react to their newfound freedom so enthusiastically. The scant minority were in stark contrast to what Lieutenant-Colonel R. I. G. Taylor, the Commanding Officer of the 63rd Anti-Tank Regiment, observed when he entered the camp. "A great number of them were little more than living skeletons with haggard yellowish faces. Most of the men wore a striped pajamas type of clothing – others wore rags, while women wore striped flannel gowns or any other clothing they had managed to acquire. Many of them were without shoes and wore only socks and stockings. There were men and women lying in heaps. Others were walking slowly and aimlessly about – a vacant expression on their starved faces." Lieutenant-Colonel was accurately describing the *Muselmänner*.

When the British entered Bergen-Belsen, they were totally unprepared for what they encountered. There were more than 60,000 emaciated and sick prisoners in desperate need for medical attention, and a horrifying 13,000 corpses in various stages of decay dotted around the camp. The soldiers' first priorities were to bury the dead, contain the spread of disease (typhus, dysentery, tuberculosis), restore the water supply, and arrange the distribution of food that was suitable for starving prisoners in various stages of malnutrition. The Dora-Mittelbau prisoners, among the last people to be sent to Bergen-Belsen, were in much better physical condition than most of the others. Some of these men sought revenge on the most abusive of their former Kapos, murdering about 170 of them the day they were liberated.

Major Dick Williams had a different experience when he liberated the camp. "This was one of the things which struck me when I first went in: The whole camp was so quiet and yet there were so many people there. You couldn't hear anything, there was just no sound at all and yet there was some movement – those people who could walk or move – but just so quiet. You just couldn't understand that all those people could be there and yet everything was so quiet... It was just this oppressive haze over the camp, the smell, the starkness of the barbed wire fences, the dullness of the bare earth, the scattered bodies and these very dull, too, striped grey uniforms – those who had it – it was just so dull. The sun, yes the sun was shining, but there just didn't seem to be any life at all in that camp. Everything seemed to be dead. The slowness of the movement of the people who could walk. Everything was just ghost-like and it was just unbelievable that there were literally people living still there. There was so much death apparent that the living, certainly, were in the minority."

The British Army immediately turned over relief operations to Brigadier H. L. Glyn-Hughes, the Deputy Director of Medical Services for the British Second Army. As soldier William Arthur Wood recalled: "We'd been trained for war wounded, we were used to terrible wounds, especially, in my case, with the facial wounds that always seemed worse than a lot of the others, and *that* we'd been trained for – how to behave and how to work. But I'm afraid when we got to Belsen we hadn't been trained for this, and it was so, so different to, well to anything. I can't explain it, it was so terrible and so different from anything we'd seen in our move up from D-Day onward. We'd seen distressed people about, people walking from town to town, but nothing like this." Glyn-Hughes and his staff were faced with the monumental task of feeding 60,000 starving people. Majer recounted: "When the Germans left Bergen-Belsen, they left lots and lots of greasy stuff in cans. Most of those who ate this stuff got dysentery."

The next day, the first deliveries of food and water arrived.

Dick Williams recalled: "The food that we'd got was just not right for these people – their stomachs just couldn't take anything. The best we could do was the tea and then we decided the best thing we could do would be to open all the tins and make a big mess of it, put as much boiling water in amongst it and make it a thin stew. This was the best we could do, so we did that – and those that could come to the cookhouses, we fed them from the cookhouses and eventually we started trying to take that service back out to those who couldn't even get that far." Majer fell into the second category. "I was so weak that I couldn't go get anything to eat."

"Some of the people were still in the huts where there were more dead than living," said Dick Williams. "We would take a [cup] of this broth and leave it at the door." (The stench and fear of disease kept him from going inside.) "We tried to do the best we could. I'm afraid sausages and beef and everything – corned beef – all got mixed up together, but at least it was some sort of liquidy food. Some people who tried to eat the real stuff straight away, it was too much and it probably killed them. But it was kindness to give them something, although it is the wrong kind of kindness."

Glyn-Hughes added: "They were full of tangled masses of people who had died slowly and painfully of starvation and disease, writhing in agony, helpless in puddles of excrement." In postwar court testimony he elaborated: "The conditions were indescribable because most of the internees were suffering from some form of gastroenteritis and they were too weak to leave the hut... The compounds were absolutely one mass of human excreta. In the huts themselves the floors were covered and the people in the top bunks who could not get out just poured it onto the bunks below."

Soldier Laurence Wand recalled: "The policy was, right from the beginning, to get people out of that awful place into proper surroundings, and you couldn't take them out until they'd been cleaned and the army had set up a 'human laundry,' which consisted of trestle tables, water supply, a clothing dump, a stretcher dump, old clothing to be discarded, fresh clothing to be provided after the inmates would be brought out of the huts, hosed down, washed down, deloused, then put into fresh clothes, and then evacuated from the camp."

Dick Williams recalled: "We set up mobile shower units where survivors could wash, have a haircut, and get rid of their lice. People in the main camp were infested with lice. If they saw that a dead person had a better jacket than they did, they would simply take the jacket and pick the lice off it."

"The primary task, of course, was to save life and to get people fed, said Laurence Wand. "To get them out of the camp into proper conditions where they could be nursed and looked after and saved from dying." The mortality rate, even after liberation, was an average of 300 to 400 deaths per day. Almost a month later, it decreased to less than 100 a day. Tragically, close to 14,000 former prisoners died a month after they were liberated.

"When we could start getting a little bit of soup, we got a bit stronger," said Max. "We realized our dream – we were not going to die hungry. We got facilities where we could change our clothes – take away the prison clothes and get clothes that were clean."

42

NOW WHAT?

As, little by little, Majer began to put on weight, he started to think about his future. He had never allowed himself this fantasy during the war. The only wish he had made in all his years in the camps was to be granted a day of food, and then to die with a full belly. He knew he was going to die, but didn't want to be hungry when death came. It was a common wish throughout the camps. But now that he had survived, the question was: Where would he go?

"While we were in Auschwitz and Bergen-Belsen, it was a dream that the world would see what one man could do," he recounted. "We believed that every country would open up for us and let us in. That they were going to do what was best for us. But that wasn't the way it was. There was the dispute over Palestine, where the Jews wanted to [go]. But the British wouldn't let them in."[1]

"Most of the people didn't want to go back to Poland," said Max, who had changed his name from Majer to Max when he arrived in Belgium as a Displaced Person. "I knew I had nobody. Where was I going to go?"

On June 22, 1945, President Harry Truman requested Earl G. Harrison, the newly appointed American delegate to the Intergovernmental Committee on Refugees, to prepare a report on the displaced Jews in Europe. Harrison made a three-week inspection tour of the Displaced Persons (DP) camps and presented his findings to President Truman.

"Generally speaking [...] many Jewish displaced persons and other possibly non-repatriables are living under guard behind barbed-wire fences, in camps of several descriptions (built by the Germans for slave-laborers and Jews), including some of the most notorious of the concentration camps, amidst crowded, frequently unsanitary and generally grim conditions, in complete idleness, with no opportunity, except surreptitiously, to communicate with the outside world, waiting, hoping for some word of encouragement and action in their behalf..."

Max attempted to take matters into his own hands rather than wait for the British to decide his future. With a friend, "We escaped from Bergen-Belsen and we went to another town – Magdeburg, Germany, a very big town, where all the Jews began to concentrate." Bergen-Belsen, now a DP camp, was still surrounded by barbed wire, though the lethal electricity no longer flowed through the fence. How could the British be so insensitive as to make people who had suffered unimaginable cruelty live behind barbed wire? Max had his own opinion. "Maybe to control the spread of sicknesses." But he'd had enough of being confined. In Magdeburg, though, "The British occupied it, and they made the decisions." Their decision was to put Max on a train for the Netherlands. From there he ended up in a Belgian DP camp.

"I reminded myself that my mother had a sister in Belgium. I started getting the idea of who I was. I had two cousins who were in the Resistance, and they survived. They came and I told them who I was. They took me out of the camp and I went to Liège (97 kilometers east of Brussels). The only job I could get was to make rubber. It was very hard work. I couldn't stay there. So I went to Brussels."

In Brussels, Max went straight to the Jewish Federation for assistance. Soon, he had a place to live and a job as a waiter at a club operated by the *Yiddische Bund*, a Jewish Socialist organization. "The Belgian people were very good to us. They gave us their rations. They gave us coal. We got train transportation for nothing and cinemas for nothing." One day, Max was waiting tables when a familiar-looking woman came in. Being one of only about 40 survivors from Zelów, this was the first time since liberation he'd seen a face he thought he recognized from Poland.

---

1. This was because in May 1939, Britain had restricted Jewish immigration to Palestine in order to gain the support of the Arab states in the war against Germany. After the war, Britain continued to block the attempts of Jews who tried to immigrate illegally, despite what they had suffered. This conflict did not end until the founding of Israel in 1948.

43

ROSA LOOKS FOR CHARLES

By July 1945, Rosa and Celina were in the American sector of Germany receiving medical care and "fattening up" at a resettlement camp. By October they were back in Brussels, having obtained an apartment together and financial assistance from Jewish relief organizations. Rosa's Belgian passport had been destroyed by the Nazis and she was considered stateless. She immediately reached out to the Belgian National Tracing Bureau to see what she could learn about Charles's whereabouts. In early October, she received a heartbreaking and perplexing response. Beside the item *Date and Spot of Last News*, someone had written: "27/2/45, near Hannover by Hermann, called Bernar VI." Next to *Death Announced By*, it was abundantly clear that Charles had not survived: "Would have been killed at the end of February 1945, near Hannover, by Hermann, Transport XXIII of Malines."

This was and still remains a vexing response that could have several meanings. I tried various avenues to try to solve it. Could a survivor named Hermann, on the same transport from Malines, have witnessed my father's death? And was Hermann a first name or a surname? To that end, using the list of people from Transport XXIII,

I looked for information on the wartime whereabouts for every man with the first or last name *Hermann* to see if one of them was in Hannover with my father. Unfortunately, the search yielded no results. I did the same with the name Bernar. Who or what was Bernar VI? I still have no idea. Could *Hermann* have been a place, for example, "near Hannover by Hermann"? That was also a dead end. I could not find a city or town near Hannover called Hermann.

Next to *Death Announced By* was a follow-up item: *Eventual Proofs*. Whoever filled out the form at the Tracing Bureau chose to save time by simply drawing an arrow to *by Hermann*, leading me to surmise that Hermann was a person, not a place. Places don't give proof, people do. It makes me want to go back in time and smack whoever filled out that form.

The results from the Tracing Bureau were in no way a definite accounting of what happened to my father. I'm sure they caused my mother to hold on to some hope that one day there would be a knock on the door, and when she opened it, Charles would be standing there, dressed to the nines, holding the ever-present cigarette between his elegant fingers.

44

A REUNION

The previous year, Allied troops had crossed the Belgian border at various points on September 2. The liberation process was rapid. Within ten days, a large majority of the country was free. It was finally safe for the Decraenes to bring me back to live in Brussels. I was now over three years old. My shiny brown curls with their ever-present, colorful ribbons, had grown into fat ringlets. They were the first thing to go. Back in my old home, I received a new wardrobe and a very short haircut. My dresses and bows were replaced with short pants. There was no talk of "Now you're a boy," because the Decraenes had never referred to me as a girl; my gender had never been discussed. Being so young, I accepted my new look and didn't ask any questions. It all seemed completely normal to me. The decisions adults made on my behalf were trusted without question.

I missed the farm but was very happy to be living with *Maman* and Papa full-time again. I resumed my favorite activities, such as visiting Parc Josaphat to feed the ducks, climb its trees, and visit the mini zoo. My peaceful existence was to be short-lived, however.

One day, a woman I didn't know came to the door. This wasn't odd, as it was not unusual for us to have visitors. Maman and Papa seemed to know her very well. She was small, with thick, dark, wavy hair. She wore a blue dress and carried a purple purse.

"Give Rosa a hug and kiss, Jean-Pierre," Maman instructed me gently when we were all seated. I did so willingly but the woman squeezed me too tightly and I felt a moment of discomfort that passed as soon as she released me.

"These are for you, Jean-Pierre," Rosa said, handing me a box of Leonidas pralines. How had she known those were my favorite?[1] The adults visited while I enjoyed my sweets and played with my toys, largely ignoring them. The talk of grownups did not interest me. Every once in a while, I looked up and found Rosa staring at me. Her smile went across her whole face, it was so big.

The visit came to a close and Rosa left. Maman and Papa told me that she was a dear, old friend of our family who had suffered a lot from les Boches. To me, Rosa didn't seem like a woman who had suffered; she had smiled so much. A few days later, Maman asked me if I remembered the lady in the blue dress who had brought me the nice box of chocolates. This was a silly question. Of course I remembered her!

"Come sit down, Jean-Pierre," said Maman, beckoning me to the leather couch where Papa was sitting. I walked over and Papa settled me on his lap. He looked sad. Maman's eyes were shiny. "We love you very much," she said. Of course I already knew that. Then she told me something I didn't know. Something I didn't want to believe.

"Rosa, the nice lady, who was just here, is your real mother," Maman said. "Les Boches took her away during the war. But before that happened, she and your real father gave you to us when you were a little baby so we could keep you safe in case anything happened to them."

I looked to Papa to see if Maman was making up a story, but he confirmed that she was telling the truth. Rosa was my real mother. I would have to go live with her soon, they told me.

I jumped out of Papa's lap and ran to my room on the third floor. I flopped on my bed and cried. I never wanted to leave this room. In its small space I felt safe. I loved my cozy bed and the pictures from the book *The Little Prince* decorating my walls. I loved the window boxes Maman filled with cheery geraniums in the springtime. I would never leave this place. Ever.

In the sanctuary of my room the nonsense talk downstairs felt like a bad dream, something I would wake up from after a few good shakes of my head. But in a few minutes, I heard Maman's and Papa's footsteps on the stairs and my fantasy ended. They scooped me in their arms and told me: "We are only your Godparents, Jean-Pierre. But it doesn't change the love we feel for you one tiny bit. We love you as much as if you were our real son." They helped me get ready for bed, and that was the end of that for the night.

The next day I woke up to the hope that the previous day's news was some kind of misunderstanding. But throughout the day, Maman peppered our talk with references to Rosa: how she had suffered a lot in horrible concentration camps, how nice she was, what a dear friend... Perhaps Maman thought she could help me warm up to the idea of accepting the woman in the blue dress as my mother. Rosa would be coming for another visit, I was told. She and Papa had made some kind of arrangement with her. Maman's talk just made me dizzy, and I shut it out.

The next time Rosa visited, I was very shy, now that I knew who she really was. She was living in an apartment with her sister that was paid for by the Belgian government. Unbeknownst to me, I had to move in with her as soon as she secured a place of her own. Until that time, she would be joining us for dinner every evening.

During the day, I put Rosa out of my mind and existed in a world of make believe. But every night when Rosa came to dinner, the reality that I would have to leave Maman and Papa and my beloved home slammed back into my thoughts.

The dreaded day came. I hid behind Maman and clung to her legs. The four of us went to the living room and sat down. It was a room I particularly loved, with its beautiful paintings, decorative statues, and comfortable furniture. My toys and clothes had already been packed. Papa and Maman cried with me, although much more quietly. "You will only be living a ten-minute walk from us, Pouyou," they reassured me, and probably themselves, too. It was arranged that I would spend most weekends with Maman and Papa, and Maman would come to Rosa's apartment every Wednesday night for dinner. These small compensations, while comforting, did not stop my tears. In less than an hour, it was over. Rosa reached for me and I had no choice but to go with her. I drew the line at holding her hand, though. After a walk of a few minutes, we reached a busy intersection. Rosa (I could not think of her as Maman) insisted I take her hand to cross the street. We reached the safety of the other side and I had no more fight left in me; my emotions had me. I kept my hand in hers. I was terribly sad, scared, and felt abandoned by the people I had always known as my loving parents.

"Don't worry," said Rosa, seeming to know my thoughts. "The four of us will be a happy family. You'll see."

Soon we reached a three-story townhouse similar to the Decraenes', but unlike theirs, Rosa only lived in one part of it. We climbed a set of stairs and entered the apartment directly into the living room. It was sparsely furnished and very clean. There was a dining table and some mismatched chairs, two upholstered armchairs with lace antimacassars across their tops, and a sofa that converted to a bed. Rosa would sleep on that and I would sleep in the little room beside the living room. I later learned that Papa had helped Rosa secure the apartment through another professor at the university whose mother, a schoolteacher named Madame Claessens, owned the building.

"Would you like to listen to the radio while I make dinner, Jean-Pierre?" Rosa asked. I told her I did, and she switched on Radio Luxembourg, which was the station that played music as well as children's stories. I can't recall what we ate, but I remember her trying to make conversation with me and I was not having it. I comforted myself with thoughts of the upcoming weekend, when I'd be reunited with Maman and Papa.

My new bedroom was as sparse as the living room. There were no pictures on the walls, just a bed with a fluffy down pillow and a small desk and chair. When it was time for me to go to sleep, Rosa kissed my forehead goodnight. I submitted to it, but I didn't respond by putting my arms around her neck the way I did with Maman.

---

1. Having had my first taste of chocolate in the recent past when the Allies gave us Hershey bars, I became an instant fan.

45

A NEW MOTHER

When I look back on that painful period, I am so thankful to both my mother and the Decraenes for the gentle path they took with my emotional well-being as they transferred me to Rosa's care. The 1940s were not a time when children's emotional health was given much thought, yet the three of them did everything they could to ease me into my new home with love and sensitivity.

Rather than being jealous of my close bond with the Decraenes, my mother was thankful that she had left me with people who had loved and cared for me with the same intensity she would have had we never been separated. Another returning mother might have thought, I'm back. Thank you very much. But I need to show him who his mother *really* is now. And who could have blamed her? But my mother never considered severing my deep connection with the Decraenes. Keeping them in my life was healthy for all involved parties. To rip me away from the people who had raised me for so many years would have been cruel to them and to me. I'm grateful to my mother for being a strong woman, secure with her place in my life. Had she not survived the war, I know the Decraenes would have told me about my birth parents when I reached the proper age to digest such news.

I spent part of that first summer at the beach with the Decraenes. I was not particularly happy when I returned to Schaerbeek and had to get used to living with my mother all over again. That fall, I was enrolled in a Kindergarten that was halfway between my old home and my new one. In keeping with the agreement, some days the Decraenes picked me up and some days my mother did. I now referred to the Decraenes as my war parents, *Marraine* and *Parrain* [Godmother and Godfather].

Intellectually, I started to accept that Rosa was my mother. I still preferred the Decraenes and I looked forward to my regular visits with them with all my might. Very gradually, though, over the span of about a year, I grew to have a loving relationship with my mother, and I became as close with her as I was with Marraine and Parrain.

But there were some difficult adjustments...

Maman cooked Jewish food, which I wasn't used to. Culturally, I was a Gentile. I remember visits to the butcher shop. Money was very tight, so Maman could afford only the cheapest cuts from the market, such as chicken feet and chicken offal, livers and gizzards, which she used to flavor her chicken soup. I hated chicken feet. Maman picked the meat around the bones which disgusted me. But I wasn't going to turn down her matzo balls or homemade noodles. Once a week she made boiled beef with kasha, an ordeal for me, to be sure. Ironically, she floated beef tongue into her regular cooking rotation and I loved that. I don't think I was aware of what part of the cow I was eating.

After we were reunited, Maman stayed home to look after me for about a year. Then she looked for a job. We lived frugally, but we could afford meals a few times a week at the Socialist Bund, where my mother sometimes attended meetings. I liked the food there. Although it was what I considered Jewish food, the cafeteria had the most delicious red cabbage. We always had the same very nice man wait on us. He seemed very interested in my mother. He'd always come to our table and tell her, "I can give you more food if you want more." He would bring me extra desserts, which I didn't care for since they were too fancy, but my mother always ate them. Pretty soon, I began to enjoy going to the Bund, more to see the nice man, whose name was Max, than for the food. My mother told me that les Boches had killed Max's entire family: his parents, grandparents, and five brothers and sisters. Despite that tragedy, Max was a great deal of fun and I liked him immensely.

The first time Max saw my mother in the Bund, he immediately recognized her. "She was from a little town beside my town," he told me. "In Poland, on Saturdays during the Sabbath, the younger generation would walk along next to one another. They had gatherings. Certain things couldn't be done at home because our parents were very religious. They were against this and that. For example, you couldn't ride a bike; you couldn't eat any food that wasn't approved," he explained. "So we had gatherings and we tried to do the best that we could. Later on, [Rosa] went from Poland to Belgium. I think she was 18 years old, maybe, when she moved to Belgium. She had a sister already living there. When I was in Belgium and I was already working in this restaurant, I found her again."

My mother had told me that on Saturdays, the young people would get together and walk up and down the main street, mirroring what Max had said. She showed me how she would walk with her girlfriend, arm in arm. I think it was a time for the guys and girls to sort of check each other out. But there is a lot about Max's recall that is unlikely. For one thing, my mother was nine years older than he was. She would not have been part of his "younger generation." They hadn't even come from the same town. Zelów was 15 kilometers from Bełchatów. In the 1930s, that distance was much greater than it is now. Especially when one factors in that at that time, in that place, there were many people who spent their entire lives within the borders of their shtetls. But the biggest reason to doubt Max's memory is that my mother was a married women with no reason to be milling around Zelów with a group of preteens. Whether it was a case of mistaken identity or not, Max latched onto my mother, and she needed him, too.

And they both needed me.

46

SETTLING IN

As more time passed without my father's return, my mother exchanged her dream of his reappearance for the reality of a life with Max. Celina had since received the devastating news that Fiszel, Albert, and Sarah had not survived. News out of Poland elicited crushing grief. Only six percent of Bełchatów's and two percent of Zelów's Jews had survived. On June 15, 1945, only six Jews were living in Zelów.

But there was good news as well. Rosa's and Celina's two half-brothers Jankiel and Herszel were alive.

Shared grief drew Max and Rosa closer. Old social rules and norms went out the window. In less than three months, Max moved into our apartment, much to my delight. He received training in the design and manufacture of women's handbags and shoes and was able to stop waiting tables at the Bund. In his new career he worked for a manufacturer at the factory, as well as from home. My mother assisted him with the handbags and delivered the orders to retail shops.

Aside from having Max living with us, there was another perk for me. Max's larger income freed me from the weekly torment of the dreaded chicken feet. Now, once a month, my mother, Aunt Celina, and I visited a local poultry farm where we selected a live bird which was killed right in front of us. Then we went home and I helped pluck the feathers. That one chicken fed us for three or four nights. (Who am I kidding? My mother probably cooked the feet.)

Food became more varied and plentiful as Max started to earn more money. On Wednesdays, when Marraine picked me up from school and spent the afternoon helping me with my homework, my mother put a lot of attention into her cooking. Parrain would join us and we'd have a festive meal. Often, Rosa would make *frites* and pork chops, because pork was so affordable. She would make Marraine, Parrain, and me swear not to tell Max, whom I now called Papa, since he'd been raised in an ultra-Orthodox family. Mama told him it was veal.

Maman and Papa showed me a lot of love, but my mother had a bad temper. If she found that I was not studying when I had been sent to my room to do so, she would scream and hit me. If Max was home, he would intercede and save me from a spanking. Maman always calmed down quickly, though, and within a few hours all was forgotten. After surviving the camps, a bit of a temper was understandable.

Rosa had lots of friends nearby, some of whom she knew before the war. We would either go to their apartments or she and Max would entertain them in ours. During one party, I wondered aloud why all the families had babies, but no children my age. My question must have caused them considerable pain.

We also saw a lot of Celina, recently remarried to a Viennese survivor named Salek Herting, who had also lost his spouse in the camps. Once a week, my mother and I visited them. Uncle Salek had an import business that dealt in toys, costume jewelry, and housewares, which he sold in Belgium, the Netherlands, Luxembourg, and

Germany. He always gave me some sort of *tchotchke*, and I loved going there. About a year after they married, Aunt Celina, at 41 years old, had a baby girl whom they named Helene.

My life had a contented rhythm. I spent Easter vacations with the Decraenes at their chalet in Wilderswil, Switzerland. Parrain and I would ski and Marraine would join us for sledding. For two weeks every summer I traveled with them to France, Luxembourg, the Netherlands, and Italy. My mother began renting an apartment for six weeks every summer in the Belgian beach town of La Panne, close to the French border. We had great fun together, but since she didn't know how to swim, she was always afraid I would drown. To scare me from going out too far, she'd tell me that's where the sharks swam. My aunt Celina rented a place in the next town, Saint Idesbald, and we all spent a lot of time together. Papa joined us on the weekends, during which time we couldn't eat shrimp, which he called worms.

Max and my mother, reinstated as a Belgian citizen, married in 1948. Since he was now married to a citizen, Max's working papers were extended a few times. But by 1952, his time in the country was over. Belgium had been flooded with refugees after the war; he would have to emigrate. My parents had concerns about staying in Europe. Max admitted in his postwar testimony that, where my mother was concerned: "Belgium was very good to her [but] it was not like the dream that we were dreaming – that there would be no more antisemitism. We saw that there was no end to it." They considered Argentina, Australia, and Israel, but ultimately settled on emigrating to the United States, "for a better future for a child," said Max.

There was another reason, too. My uncles Jankiel (who was now Jack) and Herszel (now Harry) had left for the United States in 1950 and were living in Brooklyn, New York.

Max left for the US in 1952 and stayed with Jack. My mother and I applied for a visa and stayed at our home at 12 rue Joseph Coosemans in Schaerbeek, less than a half kilometer from Parrain and Marraine. I attended the Athénée Royal de Schaerbeek, a combination middle school and high school. I continued to spend weekends with my war parents, either traveling or visiting Bomma in Vilvoorde.[1] I missed Max and was hoping that he would dislike the States and return to Belgium.

I got part of my wish. Max hated New York. "Brussels was such a nice, clean town. They would wash the sidewalk and they would wash this and that. You could not go into someone's house with your shoes on; you had to take your shoes off. I would look at Brooklyn – I wouldn't say Manhattan – and I saw so much garbage in the street and I asked myself, Is this the United States? It's packed with people and there's lots of garbage. I had been there for about two weeks..."

Soon after arriving in the New York, Max attended a shoe show in Manhattan where he met a factory owner from Fort Worth, Texas named Nathan Rakoover. Rakoover offered him a job at his Texas Sandal Manufacturing Company. Max was more than happy to leave New York. Fort Worth, at that time, was "just a little town – very little. If you looked on the map, you couldn't find it." This suited him, with his shtetl roots, perfectly well. The Jewish Federation, the human services organization found within most metropolitan areas in North America, paid his fare to Texas. When Max reached Fort Worth, he was happy with what he saw there. "It was very quiet, clean, and the pace of life in Texas wasn't too rushed then. You could take your time. What people expect done in ten minutes now, then you could take an hour to do. So I decided to stay there."

In the summer of 1954, I traveled with Parrain and Marraine to France and Italy and had a wonderful time. When we returned to Belgium, my mother informed me that our visas had come through and soon we would be moving to the United States to join Max. Once again, my life was being yanked out from under me. October 1954 was a very sad time. During my final weeks in school, I promised my friends I would write and they promised to write back. I spent the summer visiting my war relatives and endured emotional goodbyes. Marraine assured me that she and Parrain would visit me in the States.

In November 1954, my mother and I boarded the SS Ryndam of the Holland-America Line. I met some other teens from Belgium and France on the ship and enjoyed hanging out with them. They, too, were emigrating to the United States, and we commiserated with each other about leaving behind everything that was familiar to us.

When the ship sailed into New York harbor, we were met by Uncle Jack, who took us to his home in Brooklyn. He had spent several years in Brussels after the war working as a carpenter and had built me a sled for my tenth birthday. It was good to see him again. I also met his wife, my Aunt Hanka, and his children, my cousins Goldie and Henry.

After a few days, Uncle Jack took us to Woodbine, New Jersey to see Uncle Harry, who owned a chicken farm. Uncle Harry put me to work collecting and processing eggs. He even allowed me to drive his pickup truck. I had never seen one before and referred to it as the car with the open *tuchus*, Yiddish for rear-end. All in all, I started to enjoy the United States, despite missing Parrain and Marraine terribly.

We returned to New York and a few days later boarded the train to St. Louis, Missouri, where we changed trains for Fort Worth. Max, accompanied by his friend Saul Frydman, a fellow survivor who owned a car, met us at the station and brought us home to our first apartment. Our arrival was big news to the Jewish community and over the next few days, many people came and brought us food, clothes, and other items they thought we could use. I became lifelong friends with several of the teens, including Harry Bailin and Arnold Gachman.

All of a sudden, the adventure and excitement of our journey ended and life got real. My mother took me to Rosemont Junior High School and registered me. I had to endure starting junior high school two months after the term had begun. What's worse, I couldn't speak a word of English. Of course, none of the kids knew a word of French, either. Because of my language deficit, I was placed in seventh grade instead of the eighth grade I had left in Belgium. There was one bright spot, though. The football coach found out that I had played soccer in Belgium so he made me the kicking specialist on the football team.

My schoolmates welcomed me by making fun of my name, pronouncing it like the American girl's name that it is: *Jeanne* Peter. I hated that. One day I was watching a movie on television and one of the characters was an affable gangster named Harry. I immediately liked the way that sounded and decided that would be my new name. When Max formally adopted me, I legally changed my name to Harry David Pila. (Rosa also changed her name to Rose). Being adopted by Max and us all having the same surname made me feel like I was part of a real family – a real American family.

It took me only about two months to master English. But one day, before I was fully fluent, I had to give an oral report for the book *Moby Dick*. I still had a bit of an accent, but I thought I was doing pretty well until I had to talk about a seal. I couldn't remember the English word for seal, so I inadvertently blurted out the word for it in French, *phoque*. This evoked howling laughter from my classmates. I looked quizzically at the teacher for an explanation. Her face was bright red. After class, my only friend at the time, a Mexican-American who had taken me under his wing, asked me, "Do you know what you just said?"

And that's how I learned about the F-bomb.

My father was doing well in his job and six months after arriving in Texas, we moved to a larger apartment, which we only lived in for six months. My father fulfilled part of the American Dream after less than five years in Texas, when he bought the single-family house he and my mother would live in for the rest of their lives. Because our new home was in a different part of Fort Worth, I had to change schools, enrolling at McClain Junior High. Now that I was fluent in English, I was able to skip eighth grade and go straight to ninth, making up the year I had lost. I also became the kicking specialist at my new school. McClain was in a part of Fort Worth where more Jews lived, and my new friends introduced me to Aleph Zadik Aleph [AZA], a Jewish youth fraternity that was founded in 1924. I enjoyed the activities, dances, and travelling to AZA chapters in other cities. I began to fall in love with my new life in Texas.

After graduating from McClain, I started tenth grade at Paschal High School. I was living the dream as a kicking specialist at a football-obsessed Texas high school. But as I looked at my friends on the team that fall, I couldn't help but notice that they had all grown substantially over the summer, while I was still the same five feet, six inches. I feared that the other teams would destroy me on the field, so I made the painful choice to quit football and joined the swim team instead. I have wonderful memories of Paschal High School. There was never a hint of antisemitism. I made wonderful non-Jewish friends with whom I am still in touch, and had a very active social life. When I went out, my mother was always worried that I would get home late at night. To assuage her fears, I dutifully came home by midnight in our family's green Studebaker. I would say goodnight to my parents, go to my room on the other side of the house, wait a few minutes, and then sneak out the window. Two blocks away, a friend would be waiting for me in his car. I regularly re-entered the house at 2 or 3 in the morning. I never got caught.

In the summer of 1958, I went back to Belgium and lived with Parrain and Marraine for a while, working as a guide at the United States Pavilion at the World's Fair. I dated a Russian girl named Marilla who was a year older. We had a wonderful time together and never discussed politics. Before returning to the States at the end of the summer, Parrain and Marraine took me on a two-week trip to France and Switzerland. It was to be my last summer with my dear

Parrain. He passed away in October 1959. I was heartbroken to miss his funeral and not be there to support Marraine, but I had just started college at the University of Texas at Austin. (I had also been accepted to Tulane and Rice, but could not afford the tuition to those private universities.) As an in-state student, tuition at U of T was only $50 a semester, not including room, board, and books. I pledged the Jewish fraternity Tau Delta Phi, to the disappointment of my Gentile friends.

In 1962, I returned to Belgium for the summer to work at the United States Embassy, a job arranged for me by one of Parrain's friends. On the ship to Le Havre, France, I met and fell in love with a girl named Susan, whom I was determined to marry. When my summer job ended, I rented a Vespa scooter and traveled day and night over the Alps to Italy to join her and the girls with whom she was traveling. I arrived in Rappallo, where, according to their itinerary, they were staying. Unfortunately, I learned that they had not liked the town and had gone on to Rome. Undaunted and determined, I got back on my scooter and went on to Rome. I must have been a sight when I got there. I'd had no sleep and was covered with 24 hours of dirt and grease. Susan immediately told me to take a shower.

Two days later, Susan agreed to part from her friends. I had the overtaxed Vespa serviced and we motored out. We tried to get married in Lucerne, Switzerland but the Swiss Rabbi would not perform the ceremony unless Susan had written permission from her parents. On July 16, 1962, our marriage vows were witnessed by the equivalent of a Justice of the Peace in Zurich, since that city only required permission from the United States Consulate and a groom who was over 21.

We told no one what we had done. Susan's mother had fantasized about having a lavish wedding for her daughter. When we got back to Brussels, where my mother was visiting Celine, my mother told me that she thought I should be a doctor and my "girlfriend" would be a distraction from my medical studies. She tried to bribe Susan into "getting lost," with a diamond watch. Aunt Celine, who took to Susan immediately, gave Rose hell.

My bride and I traveled back to the US together on the Hanseatic of the Hamburg America Line. There was a hurricane at sea. During the storm, there were only ten people at dinner. All the tables and chairs had been chained down and the bottoms of the glasses had suction cups so they would not slide off the tables. Susan spent the storm with her head down the toilet. When we got back to New York, her parents greeted us at the dock and took us to their home. A few days later, Susan learned that her seasickness was, in fact, not seasickness at all. She was pregnant with our son, Jay. We had no choice but to tell Susan's parents that we had gotten married. Susan's father immediately said that he could arrange to have the pregnancy fixed. "Over my dead body," I told him. I'm happy to write that from that day on, we became as close as two men could be. Susan and I had a religious ceremony with her rabbi in Elizabeth, NJ, for which my parents flew in. My new mother-in-law threw us a party. My mother, though, was still having trouble digesting that we had married at such a young age, and so soon after meeting.

We flew back to Texas so I could resume my studies. To support my new wife, I taught conversational French at the university, as well as to groups of Peace Corp volunteers going to French-speaking African countries. I also worked for *Look* magazine managing groups of teenagers selling magazines door to door. Susan worked as a legal secretary for a law firm specializing in real estate.

Jay was born on April 24, 1963. My mother fell in instant love with her new grandson, relishing her time with the baby, and perhaps recalling having to give me up so soon after giving birth. Happily, by the time Jay arrived, Susan and my mother were quite close.

I graduated in 1966 with a degree in International Business and accepted a job with Shell Oil in Houston. By this time, Susan was missing her family and friends in New Jersey, so I requested a transfer east and worked out of the Trenton, New Jersey office. Shell had promised that after a year or two, I would be transferred to an overseas job in Europe, however I learned soon after my transfer that this was not going to happen, so I resigned.

I joined J. Gerber and Company, a member of the Gerber-Goldschmidt group, a global import-export company. After two years, one of my clients, Ethical Products of Newark, New Jersey, offered me the position of Director of Imports at a substantially higher salary and I accepted. I began traveling extensively to Asia to buy pet supplies. Once we were settled in our new home in New Jersey, Susan accepted a job as a dental assistant at a clinic which served underprivileged children.

In 1970, J. Gerber got back in touch and offered me a substantial salary increase to relocate to Taiwan and open their office there. It had always been my dream to work overseas. Susan packed our belongings and with seven-year-old Jay, we embarked on the adventure of moving to Taipei in November 1970. We thoroughly enjoyed living in Taiwan, even though at that time it was still a developing country. It was easy to make friends with other expats. We found the Taiwanese people extremely hard working and very friendly. In the early 1970s, Taiwan was a "benevolent dictatorship." Chiang Kai-shek was still running the country. There was total economic freedom but politics were tightly controlled. We would, in the future, see many political changes leading up to Taiwan becoming a true democracy.

In 1973, a close friend from J. Gerber and I discussed going into business together. By coincidence, the management of the company, whose average age was probably 75, decided that as a result of President Richard Nixon taking the dollar off the gold standard, imports into the United States would die and the country would become a major exporting nation. David and I knew that they were wrong. J. Gerber was happy to sell us the Taiwan company and they appointed us as their exclusive agents. We asked the CFO to join us as a minority partner; she had great connections. This was the birth of our company, Tradepower, which was eventually expanded into many offices throughout Asia, with sales offices in the United States, the United Kingdom, and South Africa. We became the buying agents for large manufacturers, wholesalers, and retailers in the US, Canada, South Africa, and Europe. In 1974, my partner moved to Hong Kong and established our head office there. Susan went to work for a Lebanese friend who owned a freight forwarding company. She established a travel department and hired several other expat wives. Hers became the overwhelmingly preferred agency to handle all of the expats' travel needs, both corporate and personal.

In January 1979, the United States established full diplomatic relations with mainland China and de-recognized Taiwan as being the Republic of China. It just so happened that we were at the last United States ambassador to Taiwan's home for a cocktail party the night this happened. I knew something was going on, as one of the ambassador's aides appeared to tell him he had to go to the embassy to speak on a secure telephone.

As a result of Taiwan's de-recognition, there were constant teacher changes at Jay's school, The Taipei American School. This occurred because most of the diplomatic personnel and military had left, which created budget constraints. As a result, we took him back to the United States to visit several boarding schools. We chose The Peddie School in Hightstown, New Jersey. After getting our son settled in, Susan and I returned to Taiwan. Jay returned to Taiwan during most school breaks. When that wasn't possible, he visited my parents in Texas or Susan's parents in New Jersey.

By 1981, Susan and I felt that 11 years as expatriates was long enough. We missed Jay and our parents, and Susan's sister, Nancy, and her family. I arranged to work out of our New York office, visiting existing and potential new customers. In time, I grew tired from the pressure of constant travel. I sold my Tradepower shares to my partners in 1983. It was time for something new.

I joined Gemini Industries, one of my prior clients, where I initially worked as a consultant. Then the CEO made me a very generous offer and I joined the company as Director of Imports. One year later I was promoted to Vice President. Ironically, I again traveled extensively to Asia doing new product development and eventually built a team of ten people. The company did exceptionally well.

Jay graduated from Boston University and married Cindi Augarten, whom we loved dearly. They had two children, Arielle and Ross, who brought Susan and me so much joy. And then the unthinkable happened. In September 2003, Cindi died suddenly from a saddle embolism following a routine hernia operation. She was only 37 years old. Susan and I immediately moved into Jay's house to provide the kids with the love and continuity they needed, and to allow Jay to work. His grief was staggering. While his career offered some distraction from his suffering, it wasn't enough. He joined a grief support group and met a lovely woman, Jill, who had lost her husband in the towers of the World Trade Center on September 11, 2001. She was pregnant with their second child when her husband was killed.

Jay and Jill married in 2004, which gifted us double the grandchildren and a much beloved new daughter-in-law. The transition was difficult, but Jill put her heart and mind into making her blended family a loving unit, and it worked out wonderfully. Both Jill and Jay deserve much credit for the way they handled the situation.

In 2004, Philips Electronics bought Gemini. I stayed for two years to help with the transition before retiring. The new freedom allowed me all the time I wanted to spend with my new, larger family.

Jay is an extremely successful consultant helping small and medium-sized businesses grow and increase their profitability. Jill is a children's speech pathologist, with degrees from the University of Michigan and Columbia.

We love all four of our grandchildren dearly. They really have completed us. Arielle graduated from the Savannah College of Art and Design and is a successful fashion designer in New York City. Nicole graduated from the University of Michigan and works in New York City in management for a Swiss company. Ross graduated from Ohio State University. He also works in New York City, handling logistics for a British company's newly established USA office. Our youngest granddaughter, Jamie, a talented snowboarder, was due to begin her studies at the University of Colorado, Boulder, but chose to defer her freshman year due to Covid-19. She took a gap year in Israel, where she fell in love with the country and the people. She decided to make *Aliyah* [immigrate] and join the Israel Defense Forces. You can only imagine how proud we are of her. I have always felt that if Israel had existed prior to 1939, the Holocaust would not have happened.

Since my retirement, Susan and I have spent more time at our home in Florida, and we enjoyed many cruises until Covid-19 halted our travels. We cruised and traveled often with our friends, Linda and Hal Gottschall. Hal was a hidden child in the Netherlands whom I had originally met in Korea. They also lived in Taiwan during our time there and we became fast friends.

I have been involved with the Holocaust Council in New Jersey. Hitler and his henchmen tried to kill us all. But we have the last laugh, as we are thriving! Despite colon cancer surgery in 2018 and a diagnosis of multiple myeloma necessitating major neck surgery in January 2021, I am doing very well, thanks to the exceptional, loving care of Susan, who went above and beyond. She even cooked for me, and she hates cooking!

---

1. Bompa had succumbed to stomach cancer.

47

POSTSCRIPT

PART 1: LEARNING THE TRUTH

In January 2020, I went to the library at the USHMM and requested information on Malines. Back in 1996, Belgium had opened The Jewish Museum of Deportation and Resistance (JMDR). One of the institution's goals was to digitize all the archival collections related to the Holocaust in Belgium, and to make these documents available to the public. Nine years later, the museum launched the *Give Them A Face* archival project, digitizing photographs of all Jewish, Roma, and Sinti deportees who passed through Malines from 1942 through 1944. More than 18,500 photos of deportees were digitized.

In 2008, the JMDR was reorganized and became the Kazerne Dossin Memorial, Museum and Documentation Center on Holocaust and Human Rights. One year later, all the photos of the digital collection were published in a four-volume commemorative book, *Mecheln-Auschwitz, 1942-1944.*

Within minutes of my request at the USHMM, a librarian placed that book in my hands. Excitedly, I turned the pages searching the R's for Russ, expecting to find my mother. Instead, I came upon a sepia portrait of Szapsa Russ. That was the moment I learned my father's true name – undoubtedly Yiddish. Catholic parents did not name their children Szapsa. A turn of the page showed a facsimile of the original Transport List where I found my father's name and two more nuggets of truth: his birthplace, and the fact that he'd been deported to Auschwitz. My mother had never mentioned that. She'd always insinuated that as a non-Jew, he had been in only POW camps, never concentration camps.

Below my father's name was my mother's: Ruchla Laja Russ Sat. A thin blue line had been inked across RUSS. When I asked the librarian why, she told me that in Belgium, for purposes of records, it was common to list a married woman's maiden name. That's why I had found my father's picture, not my mother's when I had been looking for RUSS. It was a coincidence that the next alphabetical name after RUSS was SAT. On the transport list, Szapsa was number 234 on the list; Ruchla was 235. They had been deported together, contradicting her story that she never saw him again after she was arrested.

The librarian retreated. With shaking fingers, I found Aunt Celina, Uncle Fiszel, and my cousins Sarah and Albert. Being able to "Give Them A Face" for the first time, as the archivists of the collection intended, was a very emotional experience. I never dreamt that I'd have access to such personal documentation. I had expected to see records that would support what I thought I already knew.

Learning that my father had been in Auschwitz helped me to complete the puzzle of the rest of his path throughout the war. Although I was shocked to learn he was in so many camps, I didn't question any of the records' validity. I knew they were accurate, even though I was shocked by what I learned from them.

Closing out my parents' Holocaust files was the copy of my mother's application to the Belgian National Tracing Service in regard to the fate of my father, which she filed soon after her return to the country. On the form, she listed his name as Szapsa, noting that

Charles was his *nom d'emprunt*, his nickname. This proves that my mother knew my father was Jewish. Just as she'd traded Ruchla for Rosa, Szapsa had refitted himself with a name that bolstered his assimilation in Belgium. She also identified his birthplace as Piotrków, Poland.

One thing I couldn't wrap my head around, though, was that my father had been Jewish. Learning of the camps he had been in didn't alter my sense of identity, but learning of his Judaism did. Even though I have lived my life proudly as a Jew since rejoining my mother, in terms of my sense of self, I still felt half Catholic. It's hard to let go of a part of yourself after almost 80 years. A friend suggested I take a DNA test. Even when the results showed that I was 100 percent Ashkenazi Jewish, it was hard to shake my lifelong self-recognition of being half Catholic.

As for my mother maintaining these fictions about my father – I will never know why she did that. I've heard accounts of survivors who lied about their ages during Selektions on the Judenrampe, either making themselves older or younger in the hopes it would save their lives. After the war ended, many survivors hung on to those birth years; they had brainwashed themselves so thoroughly. I searched for books and scholarly articles on the phenomena of survivors maintaining mistruths after the threat of death is gone, but I couldn't find any.

I don't think my mother was being intentionally deceitful with me. I'm sure she had her reasons for maintaining those narratives. Again, perhaps the stories she invented to protect herself and her loved ones were hard to part with. I strongly believe my mother thought I'd be safer in this world if I believed I was only half Jewish.

My mother lived through the most evil event in human history – an event that, at the time, many people around the world said could not be true. There are still people who, incredulously and despite many millions of pages and photos to the contrary, say the Holocaust didn't happen. And today, all one has to do is open a newspaper to see that not nearly enough has been learned by the lessons of the past.

Perhaps Rosa's survival of and witness to the Holocaust gave her the unique perception, surely shared by many survivors, that if the Holocaust could happen once, it can happen again. After all, Jews have been scapegoats for the world's ills throughout time.

48

POSTSCRIPT

PART 2: MORE ANSWERS

My USHMM findings brought to light my parents' Holocaust paths, but yielded just as many questions about their life together before the war. Where had they met? When had they met? When had they married, and where? When had they left Poland? Had they left together or separately?

Their camp records also revealed that my mother certainly knew my father's true religion. He would have been circumcised. Catholic Poles did not follow that practice.

I decided to hire a Jewish genealogist. With Eric Feinstein's services, I hit the jackpot. Eric reached deep into the past and furnished me with over 300 pages of records from Poland and Belgium. This bounty gave me a more detailed picture of my father, as well as his life with my mother.

I learned that my parents kept up with Belgium's visa application system every year, which granted them permission to stay in the country until January 1942. On December 27, 1940, my parents had dutifully registered as Jews, as had been decreed by the Nazis two months before. After July 1941, their identification cards were stamped in the top right corner in red, JUIF-JOOD. They reapplied to renew their visas in September 1942; their records end there. Less than two years later, they were arrested.

EPILOGUE

Carl Clauberg was arrested by the Soviet authorities, tried, and sentenced for his crimes related to sterilization. During his trial, he testified that the injections caused "no pain" because cocaine had been added to the solution, which had an anesthetic effect, and the only damage that could occur was infertility. He was released in October 1955 as part of a German-Soviet repatriation agreement and returned to his hometown, Kiel, Germany, where he resumed his gynecological practice. He never expressed any remorse, instead boasting of his "scientific achievements." He was quickly re-arrested by the German police on November 21, 1955 and stripped of his medical titles and license to practice. He died in prison on August 9, 1957 while awaiting trial. It is estimated that he carried out his sadistic experiments on approximately 700 women.

Only five percent of the 25,490 Jews and 353 Gypsies deported from Malines survived the war. From Albert and Sarah's Transport II, only four people survived. From Celina and Fiszel's Transport XXIII, 100 people survived. From my parents' Transport XXIV, almost exactly one year before the end of the war, there were 148 survivors.

Of the approximately 400,000 people who survived the selection process and were admitted to the Auschwitz camps as registered prisoners, half died as a result of starvation, disease, exposure, beatings, collective punishments, and straightforward murder by means of phenol injections or Zyklon B cyanide hydrogen gas.

After Oberscharführer Walter Quakernack delivered the surviving Hannover prisoners to Bergen-Belsen, he left for Hamburg to join a combat unit, which was disbanded at the end of May 1945. He was arrested on July 5, 1945. The British Military Court sentenced him to death in June 1946 for having given the order to shoot the prisoners in the Hannover-Linden camp whose bodies were later found in the pit. He was executed by hanging on October 11, 1945. His henchman, Rottenführer Friedrich Wilhelm Rex, was sentenced to six years in prison in 1981 before the regional court of Hannover. Due to poor health, he was excused from serving any time. In 1978, the city of Hannover erected a memorial stone on the site of the camp.

Gerard Decraene received two medals after the war for his work in the Resistance. From the Belgians, he received a round pin made of red cloth, which he wore proudly on his lapel every day. The British awarded him with a medal which he framed and hung on a wall in his home.

Majer Pila was separated from his three cousins Berek, Abraham, and Josef after arriving at Auschwitz. Berek and Abraham were transferred to the Flossenbürg concentration camp. Josef Pila died in Auschwitz on November 14, 1944. Berek also perished, but there is no information about the circumstances. Abraham Pila survived the war, but sadly, Majer never learned this and the two were never reunited.

Szapsa Russ's two surviving brothers – Szmul had died in 1928 – Josef and Hersz, did not survive the war. There are no records of them. Attempts to find any living descendants of my father's family have been unsuccessful.

In trying to piece together the events of my father's death, I sent a query to the Neuengamme Concentration Camp Memorial, of which Hannover-Linden was a subcamp. I received this response:

"Unfortunately the Neuengamme Memorial [has] only [a] very few original documents, because the SS ordered all files to be destroyed shortly before the end of WWII to cover up their crimes. Sadly because of that the only document we have about Szapsa Russ is a transportation list from the deportation from Gusen to Hannover-Mühlenberg (Linden). The transport was planned and arranged for the 6 February 1945 [and] according to our database he left or arrived in Hannover on 6 February 1945. And sadly this is the last trace about him. His name does not appear in the death books of the camp infirmary. We know that 79 prisoners died in that period of the camp. But his name does not seem to be among those. For that I would assume that he died during the clearing of the camp. Maybe during the death march, or in Bergen-Belsen, or he was shot when unable to march. Sadly there is no recording about those poor people."

My mother's story attesting to his shooting by firing squad – of a lone survivor who gave testimony of the murders – mirrors the murders of the prisoners on the last day at Hannover-Linden. After the war, the Red Cross of the Netherlands recorded: "The... prisoner H. deKlepper... witnessed this massacre by hiding in one chimney of one of the camps."

Over 75 years ago, in closing my father's file, the Belgian National Tracing Bureau gave the Szapsa Russ case its final opinion. Stamped boldly on the cover sheet of his file, it reads: "UNSOLVED".

ACKNOWLEDGMENTS

Although writing is a solitary exercise, no non-fiction writer works alone. It would have been impossible to complete this book without the help of Vincent Slatt, a reference librarian and archivist at the United States Holocaust Memorial Museum. I was able to visit the research library only once before the pandemic forced the museum's doors closed. Working from home, Vincent was able to electronically send me the invaluable journal of Arthur Lehmann, which was crucial in portraying the final months of Charles's life. Vincent also answered questions that I just couldn't solve on my own.

The genealogist Eric Feinstein was instrumental in fleshing out a true picture of who Charles really was by procuring and having translated records from Poland dating back to the 1800s as well as from Belgium at the time of his move to that country. Within the first ten minutes of my visit to the USHMM, I learned that Charles of Belgium was really Szapsa from Poland, a Jew who'd been deported to Auschwitz. When I relayed these findings to Harry, his shocked response was, "But my father was never *in* Auschwitz!" For his entire life, Harry believed that his father had been killed by a firing squad in a P.O.W. camp. When Harry and I began to work together and the story he told about his father didn't make sense to me, I instructed him to take a DNA test. The results showed that Harry was indeed 100 percent Ashkenazi Jewish. Although he accepted the results on an intellectual level, it was hard for him to swallow emotionally. Harry has always lived his life as a proud Jew, but parting from beliefs he had about himself for 80 years was tough.

Finally, I wish to thank the esteemed Laurence Schram, a researcher at the Kazerne Dossin in Belgium, for not only taking a phone call from a stranger, but for agreeing to proofread the first draft of said stranger's manuscript. Laurence added her considerable expertise in making corrections, in the hopes that more people, especially those who live outside of Europe, learn more about Kazerne Dossin and the incredible work they are doing to bring a complete picture of each and every individual who was deported from there.

PHOTOS

My mother with her step-mother and father

My aunt Celine and my mother before the war

The only photograph I have of me with both of my
parents. I am eight weeks old

Eight weeks old. I am already a hidden child (May 1941)

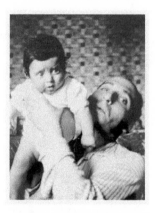

A visit from my father, two weeks after my parents gave me to the Decraenes

With my father (August 1941)

Germaine and Gerard Decraene, my "war parents"
(1938)

On the farm with my "war cousins" Simone and
Jacqueline (October 1942)

Almost 2 years old

My most feminine photograph. I am almost 3 1/2 years old

Page from a list of deportees on Transport XXIV from Malines to Auschwitz. My parents are numbers 234 and 235

The courtyard of Dossin. Kaserne Dossin Archives,
Fonds Schmidt P000419

Jewish detainees being humiliated while awaiting
deportation (1942-1944), Kaserne Dossin Archives,
Photo n° 92234 P003423

Commandant Philip Schmitt (1942-1943), Kaserne
Dossin Archives, Fonds Kummer P000749

Record that lists the name of Max and also of his
cousins who did not survive

A copy of Max's Auschwitz registration information in
which his facial features are described. His signature
appears on the lower left

In Parc Josaphat with Gerard Decraene (March 1943)

In Parc Josaphat with Germaine Decraene (March 1943)

My aunt and my mother visit me on the farm (1943)

With my "war parents" in Schaerbeek, Brussels (March 1944)

Still dressed as a girl (April 1944)

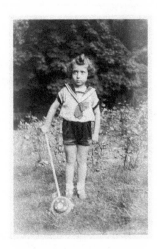

Soon after the liberation of Belgium (September 1944)

With my "war mother", Germaine Decraene, just
before my birth mother returned (3 June 1945)

With the Decraenes and my mother soon after her
return. I don't look too happy

Post-war photograph with my Aunt Celine and
my mother

Looking very much like a boy (May 1945)

With my mother and two unknown girls (8 August 1945)

With my war parents on a visit to the farm (1946)

A typical Belgian schoolboy (1947)

My adoptive father, Max Pila, showing his tattoo in an
article for the Fort Worth Star-Telegram

SOURCES

BOOKS

Auslander, Leora, Zahra, Tara. *Objects of War: The Material Culture of Conflict and Displacement.* Cornell University Press, 2018.

Awret, Irene, *They'll Have to Catch Me First.* Madison: University of Wisconsin Press, 2004.

Bauer, Yehuda, *A History of the Holocaust.* New York: Franklin Watts, 1982.

Berg, Pierre, Brock, Brian, *Scheisshaus Luck: Surviving the Unspeakable in Auschwitz and Dora.* New York: American Management Association, 2008. pp. 168-169, 191, 192, 201, 203.

Blatman, Daniel, *The Death Marches: The Final Phase of Nazi Genocide.* Cambridge: Belknap Press of Harvard University Press, 2011.

Brachfeld, Sylvain. *A Gift of Life: The Deportation and the Rescue of the Jews in Occupied Belgium (1940-1944).* Jerusalem: Hemed Press, 2007.

225

Chare, Nicholas, Williams, Dominic. *Matters of Testimony: Interpreting the Scrolls of Auschwitz.* Berghan Books, 2016.

Cohen, Judy. *A Cry in Unison.* Canada: Azrieli Foundation, 2020. pp. 57, 60, 64-65.

Deem, James M. *The Prisoners of Breendonk: Personal Histories from a World War II Concentration Camp.* Houghton Mifflin Harcourt, 2015.

Conway, Martin. *The Sorrows of Belgium: Liberation and Political Reconstruction, 1944-1947.* Oxford: Oxford University Press, 2012.

Czech, Danuta. *Auschwitz Chronicle.* New York: Henry Holt & Co. 1990. pp. 146, 151, 192, 195, 216, 290, 367.

Dean, Martin, Megargee, Geoffrey P., Browning, Christopher R., (editors). *The United States Holocaust Memorial Museum Encyclopedia of Camps and Ghettos, 1933-1945, Volume II: Ghettos in German-Occupied Eastern Europe.* Bloomington: Indiana University Press, 2012.

Deem, James M. *The Prisoners of Breendonk: Personal Histories from a World War II Concentration Camp.* Houghton Mifflin Harcourt, 2015.

Friedländer, Saul. *The Years of Extermination: Nazi Germany and the Jews, 1939-1945.* New York: HarperCollins, 2007.

Fröbe, Rainer, Füllberg-Stolberg, Claus, Gutmann, Christoph, Keller, Rolf, Obenaus, Herbert, Schröder, Hans Hermann. *Konzentrationslager in Hannover: KZ-Arbeit und Rüstungsindustrie in der Spätphase des Zweiten Weltkriegs, Teil I, Teil II.* Verlad August Lax Hildesheim, 1985.

Gilbert, Martin. *Atlas of the Holocaust.* New York: William Morrow and Co., 1993.

Gilbert, Martin. *The Holocaust: A History of the Jews of Europe During the Second World War*. New York: Holt, Rinehart and Winston, 1985.

Gildea, Robert, Wieviorka, Olivier, Warring, Anette. *Surviving Hitler and Mussolini: Daily Life in Occupied Europe*. Oxford: Berg, 2006. pp. 26, 156.

Goethem, Herman van, Alkins, Ted. *Holocaust & Human Rights*. Mechelen: Kazerne Dossin, 2012.

Graif, Gideon. *We Wept Without Tears: Testimonies of the Jewish Sonderkommando from Auschwitz*. Yale University Press, 2005.

Hakker, Joseph. *The Mysterious Dossin Barracks in Mechlin: The Deportation Camp of the Jews*. Antwerp: Excelsior, 1944.

Harfenes, Rav Yechezkel, Shapiro, Howard (editor). *Slingshot of Hell: Rav Yechezkel Harfenes' Holocaust Journal*. Southfield: P. Feldheim, 1988.

Kassan, David. *Facing Survival*. Los Angeles: ISC Fisher Museum of Art, 2019.

Knoller, Freddie, Landaw, John. *Desperate Journey*. London: Metro Publishing, 2002. pp. 197, 200, 203-207.

Koenig, Ernest. *Im Vorhof der Vernichtung: Als Zwangsarbeiter in den Außenlagern von Auschwitz*. Frankfurt am Main: Fischer Taschenbuch Verlag GmbH, 2000.

Lagrou, Pieter (2000). "Belgium", in Moore, Bob (ed.). *Resistance in Western Europe* (1st ed.). Oxford: Berg.

Lengyel, Olga. *Five Chimneys: A Woman Survivor's True Story of Auschwitz*. Chicago: Academy Chicago Publishers, 1995.

Lifton, Robert Jay. *The Nazi Doctors: Medical Killing and the Psychology of Genocide*. New York: Basic Books, 1988.

Lipkes, Jeff. *Rehearsals: The German Army in Belgium, August 1914*. Leuven, Belgium: Leuven University Press, 2007.

Marek, Anna, Urbanek, Bożena (editors). *Szpitalnictwo na Górnym Ślaski. Szpitale polskie w XIX I XX wieku ze szczególnym uwzględnieniem region Ślaska*. Katowice: Wydawnictwo Uczelni Ślaskiego Uniwersytetu Medycznego, 2016.

McAfee, Neal. *Holocaust Memories of Rosy Mandel*. Neal McAfee, 2008.

Megargee, Geoffrey P., (editor). *The United States Holocaust Memorial Museum Encyclopedia of Camps and Ghettos, 1933-1945, Volume I, Part A: Early Camps, Youth Camps, and Concentration Camps and Subcamps under the SS-Business Administration Main Office (WVHA)*. Bloomington: Indiana University Press, 2009.

Megargee, Geoffrey P., (editor). *The United States Holocaust Memorial Museum Encyclopedia of Camps and Ghettos, 1933-1945, Volume I, Part B: Early Camps, Youth Camps, and Concentration Camps and Subcamps under the SS-Business Administration Main Office (WVHA)*. Bloomington: Indiana University Press, 2009.

Michman, Dan (editor). *Belgium and the Holocaust: Jews, Belgians, Germans*. Jerusalem: Yad Vashem, 1998.

Miedzian, Myriam. *He Walked Through Walls: A Twentieth-century Tale of Survival*. Lantern Books, 2009.

Müller, Filip, Freitag, Helmut, Flatauer, Susanne. *Eyewitness Auschwitz: Three Years in the Gas Chambers*. Chicago: Ivan R. Dee, 1999.

Overy, Richard. *The Bombing War: Europe 1939-1945*. UK: Allen Lane, 2013.

Perl, Gisella. *I Was a Doctor in Auschwitz*. Lanham: Lexington Books, 2019.

Rappaport, Doreen. *Beyond Courage: The Untold Story of Jewish Resistance During the Holocaust*. Somerville: Candlewick Press, 2012.

Rosengarten, Israel J. *Survival: The Story of a Sixteen-year Old Jewish Boy*. Syracuse University Press, 2000.

Rozett, Robert, Spector, Schmuel (editors). *Encyclopedia of the Holocaust*. Abingdon: Routledge, 2000.

Schram, Laurence. *Dossin, L'antichambre d'Auschwitz*. Brussels: Éditions Racine, 2017. pp. 33, 47, 51, 52, 54.

Schreiber, Marion. *Silent Rebels: The True Story of the Raid on the Twentieth Train to Auschwitz*. London: Atlantic Books, 2000.

Selerowicz, Andrzej, Pirucka-Paul, Ewa. *The Jews of Bełchatów and Neighboring Towns*. Zelów: Rusak Marland Publishing House, 2018.

Steinberg, Maxime. *Le Dossier Bruxelles-Auschwitz: La Police SS et L'extermination des Juifs de Belgique*: Suivi de Documents Judiciaires de l'Affaire Ehlers. Bruxelles: Le Comité, 1980.

Struye, Paul. *War Diary: 1940-1945*. Root, 2004.

Suhl, Yuri. *They Fought Back: The Story of the Jewish Resistance in Nazi Europe*. New York: Crown Publishers, Inc., 1967.

Tenenbaum, Marcel. *Of Men, Monsters, and Mazel: Surviving the "Final Solution" in Belgium*. Xlibris, 2016.

Van den Wijngaert, Mark; Dujardin, Vincent (2006). *La Belgique sans Roi, 1940-1950. Nouvelle Histoire de Belgique, 1905-1950* (vol. 2). Brussels: Éd. Complexe. p. 60.

Vrba, Rudolf. *I Escaped From Auschwitz*. Fort Lee: Barricade Books, 2002.

Ward, Adriaens, Steinberg, Maxime, Schram, Laurence, Ramet, Patricia, Hautermann, Eric, Marquenie, Ilse. *Mecheln-Auschwitz*

1942-1944: The Destruction of the Jews and Gypsies from Belgium. Brussels: VUBPress, 2009.

Webster, Wendy. *Mixing It: Diversity in World War Two Britain.* Oxford University Press, 2018. p. 160.

Zaloga, Steven J. *Defense of the Third Reich in Ruins 1941-45.* Bloomsbury USA, 2012.

ORAL HISTORIES

<u>Retrieved from the United States Holocaust Memorial Museum</u>

RG-#90.063.0091, Oral history interview with Pierre Berg, Permanent Collection, United States Holocaust Memorial Museum, Washington, DC.

RG-#50.234.0008, Oral history interview with Georges Bonnet, The Jeff and Toby Herr Oral History Archive, United States Holocaust Memorial Museum, Washington, DC.

RG-#50.232.0022, Oral history interview with Luba Elbaum, The Jeff and Toby Herr Oral History Archive, United States Holocaust Memorial Museum, Washington, DC.

RG-#90.141.0032, Oral history interview with Simon Gronowski, The Jeff and Toby Herr Oral History Archive, United States Holocaust Memorial Museum, Washington, DC.

Koenig, Ernest. Jeff and Toby Herr Oral History Archive, United States Holocaust Memorial Museum. RG-50.030.0112.

RG-#50.149.0035, Oral history interview with Laurence Wand, The Jeff and Toby Herr Oral History Archive, United States Holocaust Memorial Museum, Washington, DC.

USC Shoah Foundation Visual History Archive Online

Fintz, Violetta Maio. Interview 5720. *Visual History Archive*, USC Shoah Foundation, 1992.

Penn, Linda. Interview 38042, *Visual History Archives*, USC Shoah Foundation, 1998.

Urstein, Dennis. Interview 6719, *Visual History Archives*. USC Shoah Foundation, 1995.

Weiss, Lilly. Interview 12902. *Visual History Archive*, USC Shoah Foundation, 1996.

Other Testimonies

Cohen, Judy. Interview 2003-09-03. Fortunoff Video Archive for Holocaust Testimonies. 2003.

Epstein-Kozlowski, Nechama. Interview. August 31, 1946. Voices of the Holocaust. Illinois Institute of Technology.

Handeli, Ya'akov (Jack). Interview. August 1, 2007. Norbert Wollheim Memorial.

Landwirt, Margaret. Interview. August 27, 1945. Jewish Historical Institute. Warsaw.

Raindorf, René. Interview 1992-03-20. Fortunoff Video Archive for Holocaust Testimonies. 1992.

Zimm, Alan. Interview. Virginia Holocaust Museum. 2020.

WEB ARTICLES

http://iwm.org.uk/sites/default/files/files/2018-08/Liberation_Bergen_Belsen_Transcript.pdf

http://auschwitz.org/en/history/auschwitz-sub-camps/laurahtte/

https://www.sciencespo.fr/mass-violence-war-massacre-resistance/
en/document/transit-camp-jews-mechelen-antechamber-death.html

https://encyclopedia.ushmm.org/content/en/article/Auschwitz

https://encyclopedia.ushmm.org/content/en/article/the-harrison-
report#harrisons-report-august-1945-2

https://righteous.yadvashem.org/?searchType=righteous_only&
language=en&itemId=4042684&ind=NaN

https://deportation.yadvashem.org/index.html?language=en&
itemId=5092776

https://deportation.yadvashem.org/index.html?language=en&
itemId5092783

https://deportation.yadvashem.org/index.html?language=en&
itemId=5092781

https://facinghistory.org/resource-library/text/anti-jewish-measures-
netherlands-and-belgium-between-1940-and-1944

https://subcamps-auschwitz.org/companies/

https://wiener.soutron.net/Portal/Default/en-GB/recordview/
index/105801

http://mauthausen-memorial.org

https://www.vir2biz.nl/cms2/userfiles/
vriendenkringneuengammenl/files/118870%20Neuengamme%
20Bulletin%20September%202017_v5%20(1).pdf

https://subcamps-auschwitz.org/auschwitz-subcamps/arbeitslager-
laurahutte/

http://auschwitz.org/en/history/auschwitz-sub-camps/laurahtte/

https://training.ehri-project.eu/deportation-jews-nazi-transit-camps-
drancy-france-and-malines-belgium

https://kehilalinks.jewishgen.org/belchatow

http://www.486th.org/Photos/Letters2/LHuffman.htm

PERIODICALS

Georges, Jane & Benedict, Susan. (2006). An ethics of testimony: Prisoner nurses at Auschwitz. ANS. *Advances in Nursing Science.* pp. 29. 161-9.

Hamburger Institut für Sozialforschung (ed.), *Die Auschwitz-Hefte*, vol. 1 (Hamburg, 1994), p. 101. (Translation: Lesley Sharpe and Jeremy Noakes).

JTA (Jewish Telegraphic Agency) *Daily News Bulletin*, vol. VIII. No. 234. September 18, 1941.

Kowalczykowa, J. Hunger disease in Auschwitz. Chłopicki, W., trans. *Medical Review - Auschwitz.* August 20, 2019.

From the Testimony Database of the Witold Pilecki Institute of Solidarity and Valor (Warsaw, Poland) originating from the archives of the Institute of National Remembrance:

zapisyterroru.pl/dlibra/publication/3102/edition/3083/

zapisyterroru.pl/dlibra/publication/3149/edition/3130/

zapisyterroru.pl/dlibra/publication/3582/edition/3563/

zapisyterroru.pl/dlibra/publication/3583/edition/3564/

zapisyterroru.pl/dlibra/publication/3599/edition/3580/

zapisyterroru.pl/dlibra/publication/3603/edition/3584/

zapisyterroru.pl/dlibra/publication/3605/edition/3586/

zapisyterroru.pl/dlibra/publication/3713/edition/3694/

zapisyterroru.pl/dlibra/publication/3742/edition/3723/

zapisyterror.pl/dilibra/publication/3760/edition/3741/

zapisyterroru.pl/dlibra/publication/3871/edition/3852/

zapisyterroru.pl/dlibra/publication/3891/edition/3872.pl/

zapisyterroru.pl/dlibra/publication/4095/edition/4070/

OTHER

Museum of Jewish Heritage exhibit. New York, NY, 2019

Report of the former CAMP SECRETARY Gerhard Grande to the association of those persecuted by the Nazi regime of April 9th (SAPMO-BARCH, BY 5, V 279/66)

Trials of War Criminals Before Nuremberg Military Tribunals-Washington, U.S. Govt. Print. Office, 1949-1953, vol. 1, p. 730.

Document number M-2 through M-158. Document number R-36 through R-150. Document number TC-1 through TC-93. Document number UK-20 through UK-81. Affidavit A through J. Statement I through XV. Chart No. 1 through chart No. 13. Index of documents. Chart No. 14 through 19. United States, U.S. Government Printing Office, 1946.

Letter from Viktor Brack, Oberdienstleiter, Reich Chancellery; Waffen SS, dated June 23, 1942, to Heinrich Himmler, Reichsführer of the Schutzstaffel. Nuremberg Trial Case Files/English, Evidence Code 205, Exhibit Code Prosecution 163.

Letter from Dr. Carl Clauberg dated July 7, 1943, to Heinrich Himmler. Nuremberg Trial Document 212, Prosecution Exhibit 173.

AMSTERDAM PUBLISHERS HOLOCAUST LIBRARY

The series **Holocaust Survivor Memoirs World War II** consists of
the following autobiographies of survivors:

Outcry. Holocaust Memoirs, by Manny Steinberg

Hank Brodt Holocaust Memoirs. A Candle and a Promise, by Deborah
Donnelly

The Dead Years. Holocaust Memoirs, by Joseph Schupack

Rescued from the Ashes. The Diary of Leokadia Schmidt, Survivor of the
Warsaw Ghetto, by Leokadia Schmidt

My Lvov. Holocaust Memoir of a twelve-year-old Girl, by Janina Hescheles

Remembering Ravensbrück. From Holocaust to Healing, by Natalie Hess

Wolf. A Story of Hate, by Zeev Scheinwald with Ella Scheinwald

Save my Children. An Astonishing Tale of Survival and its Unlikely Hero,
by Leon Kleiner with Edwin Stepp

Holocaust Memoirs of a Bergen-Belsen Survivor & Classmate of Anne
Frank, by Nanette Blitz Konig

Defiant German - Defiant Jew. A Holocaust Memoir from inside the Third
Reich, by Walter Leopold with Les Leopold

In a Land of Forest and Darkness. The Holocaust Story of two Jewish
Partisans, by Sara Lustigman Omelinski

Holocaust Memories. Annihilation and Survival in Slovakia, by Paul Davidovits

From Auschwitz with Love. The Inspiring Memoir of Two Sisters' Survival, Devotion and Triumph Told by Manci Grunberger Beran & Ruth Grunberger Mermelstein, by Daniel Seymour

Remetz. Resistance Fighter and Survivor of the Warsaw Ghetto, by Jan Yohay Remetz

My March Through Hell. A Young Girl's Terrifying Journey to Survival, by Halina Kleiner with Edwin Stepp

---

The series **Holocaust Survivor True Stories WWII** consists of the following biographies:

Among the Reeds. The true story of how a family survived the Holocaust, by Tammy Bottner

A Holocaust Memoir of Love & Resilience. Mama's Survival from Lithuania to America, by Ettie Zilber

Living among the Dead. My Grandmother's Holocaust Survival Story of Love and Strength, by Adena Bernstein Astrowsky

Heart Songs. A Holocaust Memoir, by Barbara Gilford

Shoes of the Shoah. The Tomorrow of Yesterday, by Dorothy Pierce

Hidden in Berlin. A Holocaust Memoir, by Evelyn Joseph Grossman

Separated Together. The Incredible True WWII Story of Soulmates Stranded an Ocean Apart, by Kenneth P. Price, Ph.D.

The Man Across the River. The incredible story of one man's will to survive the Holocaust, by Zvi Wiesenfeld

If Anyone Calls, Tell Them I Died. A Memoir, by Emanuel (Manu) Rosen

The House on Thrömerstrasse. A Story of Rebirth and Renewal in the Wake of the Holocaust, by Ron Vincent

Dancing with my Father. His hidden past. Her quest for truth. How Nazi Vienna shaped a family's identity, by Jo Sorochinsky

The Story Keeper. Weaving the Threads of Time and Memory - A Memoir, by Fred Feldman

Krisia's Silence. The Girl who was not on Schindler's List, by Ronny Hein

Defying Death on the Danube. A Holocaust Survival Story, by Debbie J. Callahan with Henry Stern

A Doorway to Heroism. A decorated German-Jewish Soldier who became an American Hero, by Rabbi W. Jack Romberg

The Shoemaker's Son. The Life of a Holocaust Resister, by Laura Beth Bakst

The Redhead of Auschwitz. A True Story, by Nechama Birnbaum

Land of Many Bridges. My Father's Story, by Bela Ruth Samuel Tenenholtz

Creating Beauty from the Abyss. The Amazing Story of Sam Herciger, Auschwitz Survivor and Artist, by Lesley Ann Richardson

On Sunny Days We Sang. A Holocaust Story of Survival and Resilience, by Jeannette Grunhaus de Gelman

Painful Joy. A Holocaust Family Memoir, by Max J. Friedman

I Give You My Heart. A True Story of Courage and Survival, by Wendy Holden

In the Time of Madmen, by Mark A. Prelas

Monsters and Miracles. Horror, Heroes and the Holocaust, by Ira Wesley Kitmacher

Flower of Vlora. Growing up Jewish in Communist Albania, by Anna Kohen

Aftermath: Coming of Age on Three Continents. A Memoir, by Annette Libeskind Berkovits

Not a real Enemy. The True Story of a Hungarian Jewish Man's Fight for Freedom, by Robert Wolf

Zaidy's War. Four Armies, Three Continents, Two Brothers. One Man's Impossible Story of Endurance, by Martin Bodek

The Glassmaker's Son. Looking for the World my Father left behind in Nazi Germany, by Peter Kupfer

The Apprentice of Buchenwald. The True Story of the Teenage Boy Who Sabotaged Hitler's War Machine, by Oren Schneider

The Cello Still Sings. A Generational Story of the Holocaust and of the Transformative Power of Music, by Janet Horvath

———

The series **Jewish Children in the Holocaust** consists of the following autobiographies of Jewish children hidden during WWII in the Netherlands:

Searching for Home. The Impact of WWII on a Hidden Child, by Joseph Gosler

See You Tonight and Promise to be a Good Boy! War memories, by Salo Muller

Sounds from Silence. Reflections of a Child Holocaust Survivor, Psychiatrist and Teacher, by Robert Krell

Sabine's Odyssey. A Hidden Child and her Dutch Rescuers, by Agnes Schipper

The Journey of a Hidden Child, by Harry Pila and Robin Black

The series **New Jewish Fiction** consists of the following novels, written by Jewish authors. All novels are set in the time during or after the Holocaust.

The Corset Maker. A Novel, by Annette Libeskind Berkovits

Escaping the Whale. The Holocaust is over. But is it ever over for the next generation? by Ruth Rotkowitz

When the Music Stopped. Willy Rosen's Holocaust, by Casey Hayes

Hands of Gold. One Man's Quest to Find the Silver Lining in Misfortune, by Roni Robbins

The Girl Who Counted Numbers. A Novel, by Roslyn Bernstein

There was a garden in Nuremberg. A Novel, by Navina Michal Clemerson

The Butterfly and the Axe, by Omer Bartov

Good for a Single Journey, by Helen Joyce

The series **Holocaust Books for Young Adults** consists of the following novels, based on true stories:

The Boy behind the Door. How Salomon Kool Escaped the Nazis. Inspired by a True Story, by David Tabatsky

Running for Shelter. A True Story, by Suzette Sheft

The Precious Few. An Inspirational Saga of Courage based on True Stories, by David Twain with Art Twain

Jacob's Courage: A Holocaust Love Story, by Charles S. Weinblatt

---

The series **WW2 Historical Fiction** consists of the following novels, some of which are based on true stories:

Mendelevski's Box. A Heartwarming and Heartbreaking Jewish Survivor's Story, by Roger Swindells

A Quiet Genocide. The Untold Holocaust of Disabled Children WW2 Germany, by Glenn Bryant

The Knife-Edge Path, by Patrick T. Leahy

Brave Face. The Inspiring WWII Memoir of a Dutch/German Child, by I. Caroline Crocker and Meta A. Evenly

When We Had Wings. The Gripping Story of an Orphan in Janusz Korczak's Orphanage. A Historical Novel, by Tami Shem-Tov

Want to be an AP book reviewer?

Reviews are very important in a world dominated by the social media and social proof. Please drop us a line if you want to join the *AP review team.* We will then add you to our list of advance reviewers. No strings attached, and we promise that we will not be spamming you.

info@amsterdampublishers.com

ABOUT THE AUTHORS

Harry Pila (Jean-Pierre Russ) was born in Belgium in 1941. He moved to the United States as a young teen, attended The University of Texas, and had a successful career in the import-export business. He lives in New Jersey and Florida with his wife, Susan.

Robin Black specializes in researching and writing Holocaust memoirs for survivors and their children. She lives in New Jersey with her husband and youngest child, where she is at work on her fourth book.

CPSIA information can be obtained
at www.ICGtesting.com
Printed in the USA
BVHW071534131022
649110BV00003B/18